3595 6415

YO-CCJ-471

Catching the Dream

A Parent's Guide for Children's Dreams

Janet S. Gould

2006

Pearson Publishing Company
Corpus Christi

Library of Congress Control Number: 2006932144

ISBN-13: 978-0-9768083-5-0, paperback
ISBN-10: 0-9768083-5-8, paperback

ISBN-13: 978-0-9768083-6-7, e-book
ISBN-10: 0-9768083-6-6, e-book

Cover art and design: Glen Partain
Cover production: Tamara Schleman of Graphics, Etc.
Book design: Katherine Pearson Jagoe Massey

Published by
Pearson Publishing Company
Corpus Christi, Texas
www.PearsonPub.US

Dedicated to

Kelley, Trevor, and Zakary

thanks for sharing your dreams with me

Dreams are a crucial part of the human reaction to family crises, natural disasters, illnesses, injuries, and other traumas.

—Alan Siegel, Ph.D. in *Dreams That Can Change Your Life*

Table of Contents

Introduction

Dreams can be considered gifts of nature which permit us to commune with our unconscious. In these unconscious ideas lies power for personal recovery and creative activity. Our greatest vulnerability also lies in our dreams, because no matter how rational we are, our unconscious seeks ways in which it can manifest itself. Although dreaming is an entirely normal part of our lives it is an often-neglected part of our mental health, which can be of positive use to us in self-understanding and overall wellbeing. Not only does dreaming reveal the unconscious part of us but also the conscious part.

If we are mindful of our dreams, the difficult course which we traverse during life can be much less harsh and anxiety-producing. When we are ready to see and listen, dreams can offer us a helpful perspective on where we have been and the possibilities that lie ahead. Dreams are the language of the soul and through our dreams we can attain an increase in self-awareness. They can also help us fulfill the whole of our potential. While often concentrating on needed growth and development, dreams can tell us what we need and what we desire in order to be complete.

Dreaming can be regarded as a fascinating window to our minds. We all dream but not all of us remember our dreams. What determines dream recall? Non-recall of dreams can be attributed to simply forgetting, a lack of interest, repression (an unconscious pushing away of difficult material), or suppression (a conscious decision on the sleeper's part not to mention a dream even though he does recall something). Research has shown that recall of dreams increases as we make an effort to remember.

Dreams come from our own heads – recent experiences, memories, thoughts, feelings, wishes, and fears. While dreaming involves a part of our minds of which we are not usually aware, it can help us uncover the hidden parts of ourselves. The content of a dream is invariably more or less determined by our personality, age, sex, class, habitual way of living, level of education, and by the events and experiences of our entire previous life. For the child as for the adult, dreaming is thinking in images during sleep, and the nature of this thought appears to be highly variable in form and significance, no less so than the thought which is carried on during wakefulness.

If we dare to look at them, dreams can be helpers, and they will teach us about ourselves. Dreams give us a safe way to let off steam. They are very useful, especially if we don't run away from them. Often they will help us sort out emotions, impressions and other ideas. They can also help to restore balance between the various parts of our personality, so that they complement rather than destroy each other. Often described as the dress rehearsal for life, dreams sometimes have surprising results.

It is important that we work with all dreams, no matter how elusive, simple or just plain silly they may seem. It's important because there are many potential payoffs for working with them. One benefit is that they can provide direct access to the key emotional issues of our lives. One of the only ways our deepest-knowing, intuitive self gets to communicate with our everyday self and its emotional issues is by sending us messages through the dream state. Those messages offer us advice, support, healing, encouragement, solutions, gratification, and even warnings. But no matter what the messages may be, dreams come in the service of health and wholeness.

So what is the purpose of dreaming? Most dream researchers agree that dreaming allows us to process experiences and feelings that are meaningful. The limbic system, the more primitive part of the brain, goes frantic with electrical activity during REM (Rapid Eye Movement) sleep (when most dreams take place), indicating a very real need for the deepest levels of the mind to go into free flow during its dreaming phase. During this free flow, the dreamer can accomplish anything - from flying, to creative pursuits, to solving problems. Studies show that REM sleep deprivation can result in emotional difficulties. Not only can dreams help us to understand ourselves, but they also help us to heal - emotionally and sometimes even physically.

Children who work with their dreams enter a magical world of wonder. They are the directors of the dream. If they choose, they can become a superhero or a fairy princess. Dreams can be used creatively in numerous ways - from writing poetry to painting masterpieces. Children of all ages can learn to interpret their dreams and how to work with them. They can also uncover any fears or problems they may be having in waking life that could be causing nightmares. By recognizing these fears children can then work out a solution and bring the nightmares to an end.

There are many benefits to taking time to explore our children's dreams with them. It helps us to communicate with each other better, improve mutual understanding and provides us with a wealth of fascinating knowledge about their beliefs and attitudes. Through our children's dreams, we are able to discover what excites and fascinates them. We may also receive valuable insight into any problems that the child may be having. Negotiating childhood can often be a major challenge for children and parents; working with dreams will often provide needed guidance along the way.

Dreams may contain ineluctable truths, philosophical pronouncements, illusions, wild fantasies, memories, plans, anticipations, irrational experiences, even telepathic visions, and heaven knows what else.

—Carl Jung in *Memories, Dreams, Reflections*

Chapter One
Different Types of Dreams

Once we start paying attention to our dreams we are often given guidance on how to proceed in many areas of our lives. Dreams can help us uncover unconscious aspects of ourselves. When we look at our dreams, we can see two types of content: manifest and latent. Manifest content is composed of the obvious facts of the dream, such as where the dream is set, any characters in the dream and the action that takes place. Latent content concerns the underlying structures and perhaps the meaning of the dream.

Ordinary Dreams

Many of our dreams can be considered ordinary dreams. They are often set indoors, frequently in houses. In our dream houses, the living room is the most popular setting, followed by the bedroom, the kitchen, the stairway and the basement (Van de Castle, 1994). We also move around in our dreams. We seem to like riding in cars the most, although airplanes and boats are also common.

According to Hall and Van de Castle (1966) ordinary dreams usually have two other characters besides the dreamer. As children and teenage dreamers, the other characters are usually the mother and father. This changes as the dreamer ages. Then spouses and children will replace parents as major characters. Talking, sitting, watching, and all other "passive" activities account for a quarter of all dream activities. We also prefer pleasurable activities rather than the humdrum business of waking life. Our dreams are often full of dancing and playing games.

Ordinary dreams can often be a rehash of daily events. Freud (1965) called this "day residue:" a spilling over into our dreaming minds of what was happening during our waking day. For example, a person who plays cards right before going to bed may continue to play cards all night in his dreams. One theory is that these dreams can help us put these daily events into our subconscious minds by processing the memories, putting the memory to rest, so to speak (Foulkes, 1962).

Six-year-old Maggie spent the afternoon at a friend's birthday party. It was a theme party and all of the little girls were dressed up as fairy princesses. There were several games played, along with singing and dancing. The birthday cake was fit for a princess and the birthday girl had a mountain of presents to open. That night Maggie dreamed of the party. Everyone was laughing and having fun, only this time it was Maggie's birthday, and she was opening all of the presents.

Guidance/Problem Solving

Dreams have an innate problem-solving wisdom, and people should be aware that they can ask their dreams for guidance, to help them solve a problem or shed light on a situation that needs clarification. One method is to write down what you want to find out on a piece of paper before going to sleep. Immediately upon waking, record the dream. See how the dream associates with the question asked before going to bed. You may have dreamed the answer or at least received some clarity on the situation. Attempting to solve a problem can increase dream recall since it creates a special reason for remembering (Reed, 1973).

One common element in this type of dream is seeing something in a new way, or making a new connection, which can be thought of as a basis of self-knowledge and ordinary problem solving. Sometimes we cannot see the solution to a problem until we have greater self-knowledge, and dreams are an excellent mirror to stimulate that kind of self-revelation. What's more, dreams are good for problem solving because, during sleep, the mind is relatively unencumbered by recent stimuli, external stimuli, intruding thoughts and lack of critical reflection (Rechtschaffen, 1978).

Twelve-year-old Elizabeth was getting ready to attend her first school dance. Her mother took her shopping for a new dress. They found so many beautiful dresses that Elizabeth just couldn't make up her mind on which one to get. Elizabeth became very frustrated so her mother suggested that she "sleep on it" and then make her decision in the morning. At bedtime Elizabeth wrote the words "which dress should I wear" on a piece of paper and then put the paper under her pillow. As she fell asleep, she thought about each of the dresses that she liked. In the morning Elizabeth couldn't really remember any of the details of her dream except that everything was pink. There had only been one pink dress that she had liked, and that's the one she wore to the dance.

Illness

Dreams can diagnose illness. *The Iliad* of Homer contains dreams of gods bearing messages, as do other ancient writings. It was believed that gods could cure illness through the medium of dreams. The physicians Hippocrates and Galen consulted dreams for both diagnostic and prognostic data. History is full of

2

references to different cultures that believed that their dreams could tell them what was wrong with them and how to heal the problem. In ancient Greece and Rome people would journey to a temple of healing where they would wait for a dream from the gods. In Native American cultures dream quests are a way of life.

Dreams can be affected by our physical condition. Robert E. Haskell (1985) has said "whatever is dreamed is real in terms of physiological responses" (p. 113). If we dream we are running, our respiration rate will probably increase. Wake up from a nightmare, and our heartbeat will most likely be racing. Psychologically, prognostic dreams can be explained in terms of subliminal perception or the dreamer's cognitive processes perceiving cues too subtle to be processed consciously. Haskell gives the following example: a man dreamed that he fell from a wharf into the water between the wharf piles. A yacht was moored alongside. The yacht squeezed him onto the pier structures. On the basis of the dream, the man's doctor administered an EEG and found evidence that the man had experienced a heart attack (p. 111).

Studies done by Hilgard (1977) indicate that there may exist a non-conscious cognitive monitoring system that registers information on the internal physiologic state of the body and represents that information in dreams. Hilgard has metaphorically termed this monitoring system as a "hidden observer." While in the dream state, the "hidden observer" monitors a person's dream construction. It does the non-conscious planning, directs the plot and gauges the length of the dream.

Dreams can also reflect an illness. For example, a man with reduced circulation in his legs dreamed of a dried riverbed; a woman with bowel problems dreamed of clogged pipes. Someone with respiratory or lung problems may dream of suffocation. A woman who has arthritis dreamed her arms were in a straight-jacket. A woman with multiple sclerosis dreamed she was trying to kill a spider. She stepped on it, but it did not die. Its legs were spread out and paralyzed, just as her legs were. For children, they may have dreams in which they feel unwell or are actually sick. These dreams could indicate an approaching illness. Sometimes it may be a dream image that is ill, such as in the case of three-year-old Tammy who dreamed that her doll was sick.

Studies have shown that people with hypertension have a higher rate of hostility in their dreams (Haskell, 1985). People who suffer from asthma or migraine headaches often see themselves in the role of a victim of aggression in their dreams. These attacks often awaken the dreamer. Studies done by Foulkes (1967) showed that vivid and bizarre dream content was most often reported by subjects with some indication of disturbance in waking personality functioning.

Rehearsal

It is possible that we can rehearse upcoming events in a dream. The rehearsal can help us deal with the event when it arrives. Dreams can be viewed as journeys into the world of thought forms. A dream can awaken a particular response pattern needed in waking life, or it can permit us a rehearsal experience with a response we already know is best (Thurston, 1978).

Rehearsal dreaming can help us improve our memory. For example, some students have found that studying for an exam right before going to bed helps them to remember the material better. While falling asleep, they continue to go over the information mentally. This brings the information straight into the subconscious mind, making it easier to retrieve in the morning. Rehearsal dreaming is also good for athletes, such as in the case of fifteen-year-old Charlie who dreams of performing football maneuvers.

Through middle and late childhood the content of children's dreams often functions as a vicarious rehearsal for developmental roles. For example, boys will dream about things their fathers do such as hunting and fishing. Girls will often dream about taking care of babies and household chores (Foulkes, 1978).

Dreams have a way of rehearsing some of the things we fear. Perhaps it's a way of experiencing things that could happen. For example, after hearing her parents have numerous fights, the child may dream that her parents are getting a divorce. Dreams introduce us to change, sometimes before it happens (Wiseman, 1989).

Release

Release dreams are our way of disposing of the everyday mental and emotional baggage that we collect. Sylvia Browne (2002) says that release dreams are usually the most confusing, chaotic, preposterous, and disturbing dreams that we experience. They are also very necessary. Some release dreams are silly and many more of them are nightmares. But without release dreams, including the nightmares, we'd all be chronically stressed out.

The nightmares tend to be about something terrible happening to ourselves or one of our loved ones or some other horrible, terrifying experience. The dreams stay with us for a long time. Release dreams are a subconscious expression of our "worst case scenario," the most awful thing we can possibly imagine - so awful that we refuse to let our conscious mind imagine such a thing for more than a moment or two before we focus on something more manageable. What our conscious minds push away as quickly as it can, our subconscious minds keep track of and act out. It's not perversion nor a matter of one side of ourselves trying to scare another side. Instead, it can be a kind of reassurance whereby if "the worst" happens, we'll somehow manage to survive it.

Release dreams can also instigate a change in our waking lives. Five year-old Timmy dreamed that his new puppy, Spike, got run over by a car. Timmy awoke sobbing uncontrollably. During the following weeks Timmy hardly let Spike out of his sight. Then, with his parent's help, they set out to make their home a safer place for Spike. They made sure that Spike didn't run around loose near the street. Timmy walked Spike on a leash. Eventually Spike and Timmy's yard was completely fenced in, making it a safer place for both of them.

Creativity

There are many historical examples of creative dreaming. Elias Howe, the inventor of the sewing machine solved the problem of the needle in a dream. There were also scientific discoveries attributed to dreams: French chemist Friedrich August Kekule found the answer for the structure of the benzene molecule (the benzene ring) in a dream about two snakes which came together in a ring by each taking into its mouth the tail of the other. In 1936, the German scientist, Otto Loewi, won the Nobel Prize in physiology and medicine. Loewi credits his dreams about frog experiments in his work on the nervous system (Baylis, 1977). Thomas Edison's invention of the light bulb came from a dream. Even Albert Einstein kept a notepad next to his bed, in order to catch the creativity that might surface from his mind at night.

Composers Mozart, Schumann and Wagner all used their dreams in creating their work. Steve Allen once performed a song on the Merv Griffin television show that he had dreamed which he titled "I Had a Dream Last Night About My Old Piano." The song "Yesterday" came to Paul McCartney in a dream, and Billy Joel claims that all of his music comes from dreams. Russian composer, Anton Rubinstein, wrote a piano concerto as a musical expression of a dream he had. Many famous writers also used their dreams such as Dante, Voltaire and Poe. *Dr. Jekyll and Mr. Hyde* was created by a dream of Robert Louis Stevenson. *Salem's Lot*, by Stephen King was inspired by a dream.

There is often creative inspiration in dreams. Twelve-year-old Sharee uses her dreams as an inspiration for writing poems. She keeps paper and a pen next to her bed so she can jot down the dream immediately. To increase the creativity in your own dreams, increase your creativity in your waking life; expose yourself to all forms of creativity such as paintings, music and poetry; and use your imagination in daydreams and fantasies. Gordon Globus (1987) says that dreams are first hand creations instead of pieced together remnants of our daily lives. Globus believes that creativity is most clearly shown during lucid dreaming.

Lucid Dreams

A lucid dream is a dream in which you are aware that you are dreaming or you become aware during the dream. In *Control Your Dreams*, Gackenbach and Bosveld (1989), explain: "Many, perhaps most, people have had instances where they suddenly realized during a dream that they are dreaming, but the thought typically dissolves quickly, overpowered by the compelling imagery of the dream. Some individuals, however, 'wake up' within the dream; they realize they are dreaming and at the same time can recall their waking lives. It is an experience rich with emotion, charged with the *wow* of a spectacular view rarely glimpsed, of an altered state of consciousness naturally induced" (p. 9). Depending on the nature of the experience, the lucid dreamer may be a passive observer or an active participant, perhaps directing the actions of the dream.

There are three main ways that lucid dreams may be triggered: feelings of fear or anxiety; some inconsistency that the dreamer notices; and the dreamer's sense of dreamlike qualities. Because lucid dreams are so clear and vivid, they are easier to remember than other dreams, down to the minute details. Lucid dreams have been reported by children as young as 3 and 4 (Hunt, 1986).

A five-year-old dreamed a dinosaur was chasing him. He inserted a can of spinach in the plot, and upon eating it gained Popeye's strength and defeated the foe. A ten-year-old dreamed that a witch was holding her and her sister in a high tower. The sisters were in a panic until the girl realized it was a dream, and she could do anything she wanted. As the witch threw the girls out the window, they laughed as they floated all the way down (LaBerge & Rheingold, 1990).

Children who read fantasy books are more likely to have lucid dreams. Studies done by Gackenbach (1991) show that recall of lucid dreams appears to go down as the child ages. Among the ten-year-olds, 63% said they had monthly lucid dreams, 58% of eleven-year-olds did, and 36% of twelve-year-olds remembered monthly lucid dreams. The reason for this decrease may be partly due to the fact that our culture usually doesn't provide encouragement for children to develop and expand their ability for lucid dreaming.

Lucid dreaming can provide a way to tap into the mind's creative powers, and they can be very therapeutic by visualizing certain beneficial outcomes to the dream. Some of the benefits may include improved athletic performance and accelerated healing. These visualizations are more effective because dreams involve the brain and body more directly than do mere imaginings. Another benefit is that characters in dreams can give the dreamer a good experience on how to handle real people in waking life (Horgan, 1994).

Hypnagogic and Hypnopompic State

The hypnagogic state is the period when we are falling asleep, the period of time while we drift off. Slow drifting eye movements and vivid, brief dreamlets characterize this transitional state between drowsy wakefulness and light sleep. There is often a feeling of loss of control followed by an increased sense of hallucinatory or dreamy imagery. Often the experienced events feel real, as if they are actually happening. Hypnagogic dreams seem to occur during a fairly short time span. The imagery may seem more like a series of snapshots than an actual dream (Van de Castle, 1994). The hypnogogic state can be used in many different ways, such as presleep suggestions; asking questions and receiving answers; and receiving messages from the imagery.

Fourteen-year-old Sam had been in the same group of friends since they were youngsters. Recently he had noticed that some of the boys had started to get a little wild. They were skipping school and had started smoking. Sam really liked these boys but he wasn't sure whether he should continue to hang out with them. He was thinking about this dilemma one night as he was falling sleep. While in the hypnogogic state, he saw a picture of his friends being arrested by the police. Sam knew that he'd have to break his friendship with the boys so that he wouldn't also get into trouble. That wasn't the kind of life he wanted to lead.

The hypnopompic state is the period of time while waking up, the state when you have just awakened and feel as though you are falling back to sleep. The hypnopompic state can be used in different ways such as receiving answers from questions asked, and receiving messages from the images. It is possible to reenter the dream during this state by resuming the sleeping position you were in when you began waking and see the dream playing in your mind. Let your mind merge with the dream images. Questions can be asked once you're back in the dream or the dream can be changed. If it was a particularly good dream, you may just want to reexperience it. Perhaps the dream wasn't finished, and you want to see how it ends.

Psychic Dreaming

In primitive and ancient societies, dreams were typically thought to be the work of supernatural entities, appearing to mortals with messages of hope or despair. It was generally believed that dreams could provide a glimpse of the future, reveal events happening at a distance or indicate the thoughts of another person. For many centuries, the recordings of purportedly paranormal dreams referred to anecdotal material (Krippner & Ullman, 1970). One such historical story is how Abraham Lincoln dreamed of his own death. Mark Twain dreamed of his brother's funeral just before his death in a riverboat accident.

Telepathic dreams are dreaming about something that is actually happening. Telepathy is the direct passing of information, knowledge, or feelings from one person to another without using any of the usual five senses of hearing, sight, touch, taste or smell. It's an instantaneous, silent transference from any subconscious "sender" to any subconscious "receiver," either with or without either of them being aware of it or deliberate about it at the time it happens. Because telepathic information is often meant to have an impact on the receiver, and is sometimes meant to be acted upon, the conscious mind is open to receiving it (Browne, 2002).

Precognitive dreams are dreams in which you actually see or experience a future event. These dreams may include entire stories or sequences of events. There are different types of precognitive dreams: some seem to be related to the planning functions of our minds, thus preview important crossroads in our lives; and still others visit scenes of physical danger in which we may be exposed to later in life.

Gillian Holloway (2001) believes that all precognitive dreams are in the interest of supplying us with greater information and resources to better handle future choices. Some of these dreams allow us to visit potential futures and give our choices a run through to learn about cause and effect. Warning dreams don't mean that the events will unfold exactly as in the dream. Instead, when the events began to unfold in waking life, the dreamer is able to recognize the situation and change the outcome.

Tyler had precognitive dreams all through childhood. He didn't realize they were precognitive until the events actually happened. Tyler wasn't dreaming about important events or warnings; they just seemed to be about normal experiences. For example, one night he dreamed he was at a miniature golf course with his family. A young couple arrived with "Just Married" written on the back of their car window. The young couple began playing golf, and taking photographs of themselves in front of the structures. A couple of years later the exact event occurred.

Recurring Dreams

When a person has the same dream over and over, it is considered a recurring dream. The recurring dreams may have minor differences, but basically it is the same dream. There is no time limit on these dreams; they may come for weeks, months, even years. There may be a space of time without the recurring dream, and then suddenly it starts up again. A recurring dream usually means there is something the dreamer needs to pay attention to or take care of and until the dreamer understands the message of the dreams they will continue. These dreams can be seen as signposts that provide signals about what the dreamer is going through and how it is impacting waking life.

Gayle Delaney (1989) says recurring dreams represent a challenging issue in the dreamer's life that has been reoccurring, something the dreamer can't get away from. The dreamer should see how the dream relates to waking life. What keeps recurring in waking life that causes the same feelings as in the dream? She goes on to say that one common recurring dream is where someone or something is chasing the dreamer. The dreamer should ask who or what have they been running away from in waking life. Once the conflict is discovered then the problem can be worked out.

Recurring dreams are quite common, and they usually explore the questions and pressures we face and our responses to those pressures. Recurring dreams may occur during particular passages in life. Different ages and different genders will usually have different types of recurring dreams. Holloway (2001) refers to these as "developmental dreams" that seem to coincide with the stresses and questions that are encountered at particular stages of life.

After being stung by a bee when she was three, Annie began to have repetitive dreams of being chased and bitten by bees and other bugs. While her parents initially assumed that the bee sting experience was still bothering her, they began to notice that Annie would get stung in her dreams when other things would upset her; when her Mom went on a business trip, when she temporarily lost her favorite doll, and just after her brother was born. Her bee sting dreams had become symbolic of events that threatened her security (Siegel & Bulkeley, 1998).

One of the most common recurring dreams during childhood is that there is something scary in the bedroom. There may be a monster in the closet or something evil under the bed. There may be someone hiding behind the door or in the corner just waiting to jump out. For younger children, they may just feel something is trying to get them. Because these dreams repeat, there is no doubt that something is bothering the child.

Sometimes the child may continue to see the dream images a few seconds after waking up. This is common and parents shouldn't be alarmed. Encouraging the child to talk about the dreams can be very helpful. Sharing a dream can easily dissipate the tension around them. Parents shouldn't try to comfort a child by saying it was "just a dream". If the dream keeps recurring, then it is likely there is something behind it to cause the anxiety. Responding with "it wasn't real" may discourage the child from sharing any dreams in the future because she isn't being taken seriously (Holloway, 2001).

Visitation Dreams And Other Dreams Of The Deceased

Visitation dreams are actual contact from the other side. The most common visitation dreams are about deceased relatives and friends that occur shortly after

9

their death. The deceased come through for a variety of reasons: to strengthen our belief in the after life, because they left some unfinished business, to offer assistance and guidance, to say good-bye (creating closure) or to offer comfort. These dreams are excellent for healing the dreamer's grief. Sometimes the deceased just wants to make contact, to let the dreamer know that they are still around.

Dreams are an easy way for the spirit world to contact us and a way for us to visit with them. Sometimes that's what the dream is, a visit from a loved one. Smells (such as the deceased's perfume), vivid colors and actual conversations may accompany the dream. These soul-to-soul contacts show us that there is continued life after death and that the loved one that has passed is still mindful of the living ones and watching over them. After having a visitation dream, there is often a feeling that love survives the grave (Thurston, 1988).

There are times when the deceased is in need of assistance. They may have died in a confusing or violent way. They may not understand that they are dead. If the family is not coping with the grief of losing the deceased one, it could cause the spirit to be in turmoil. They may need help. The best way to help these spirits is through prayer. Through prayer, the deceased and the living family can be comforted. Communication can be done mentally - through the mind, or aloud - an actual verbal conversation. It is better to let these types of dreams come spontaneously and not try to initiate or force them.

Not all dreams of the deceased are visitation dreams. Sometimes it's the attempt of the dreamer to work out some conflict with the deceased. Even though these dreams may represent an inner struggle, they are healing experiences. There could be a situation in waking life that is a reminder of the deceased person. For example, there may be some conflict that is similar or certain emotions associated to something experienced with the deceased. Through our dreams, we can seek resolution of our current issues. Some type of external stimuli that is a reminder of the deceased one could also cause these dreams. For example, the smell of roses could bring memories of a grandmother who always wore that scent. Hearing an old joke could bring memories of a funny uncle.

How can you tell if a dream is an actual visitation or just a symbolic image? One way is if the dream was scary. For example, a boy dreamed that he was with his deceased mother. The sky was ominous and huge birds were attacking them. Suddenly, other deceased relatives arrived and fought off the birds, keeping the boy and his mother safe. This dream represented the boy's fear of living without his mother. The ominous sky was symbolic of his tumultuous emotions. The relatives fighting off the birds showed the boy that he could get comfort and healing from his relatives in waking life.

10

Chapter Two
Basic Dream Interpretation

Carl Jung characterized the dream as a "drama taking place on one's interior stage." A drama is presented by means of a structure similar to that found in most dreams. A drama or dream usually has four components: (1) an opening scene which introduces the setting, characters, and initial situation of the main character; (2) the development of the plot; (3) the emergence of a major conflict; and (4) the response to the conflict by the main character (Van de Castle, 1994).

Often, in our dreams, we become a "witness," a silent witness to ourselves acting in the dream. We observe the action without comment or trying to change the situation. The witness, calm and relaxed, silently watches what we do and what we think. It's the same as when we are daydreaming. One part of us may be reading a book, or washing the dishes, and the mind wanders off to something else: a television show we want to watch or an upcoming social event. In our dreams the witness just watches. At other times, we are an active participant in the dream. We are bouncing the ball, or driving the car, or climbing the ladder. We are the star of the dream. Whether we are a witness or an active participant, there are some basic interpretation methods. Most dreams will follow typical themes, include symbols, and can be interpreted.

Typical Themes

Socialization and morality. Dreams are most often populated with at least two other characters besides the dreamer, says Calvin S. Hall and Robert Van de Castle (1966) in *The Content Analysis of Dreams.* When we are children and teenagers, our mother and father are in our dreams the most often. Once we have grown, and the significant people in our lives have changed, so do our dream characters. We then will have our spouses and/or our children, close friends, etc. in our dreams. The other people who enter our dreams are usually those with whom we are emotionally involved. The emotion may be love, fear, anger, or a mixture of more than one.

Morality is another socialization theme. This topic is especially important to the issues related to working with children and their dreams. Therefore, considerable description will be offered here of the development of the child's moral sense. Young children's ideas of right and wrong seem to be determined by what they have been taught is right or wrong, from either being told by their parents or from observing their parents' attitudes. Piaget and Inhelder (2000) refer to this as "morality of constraint." That which is wrong seems most of the time to be that which is destructive or aggressive as defined by the parents or other parental adult. Here, morality refers to the child's standards of what is right or wrong, good or bad, in evaluating someone's behavior.

A child's age will be a determining factor in morality. For example, a two-year-old will consider "bad" someone pushing, scratching, and crying. Spanking, time out, or some other equivalent method that will seem severe to the child will punish these behaviors. Bad and naughty are often associated with what seems like minor misdeeds, largely evaluated by the parent's actions (Pitcher & Prelinger, 1963).

The three-year-old on the other hand is increasingly aware of the goodness and badness of aggressive actions, particularly those which harm or damage others. Good and bad are sometimes closely associated for purposes of contrast: good and bad sharks fight; a bad bear got into a good bear's bed; the boy got a new dog – a good dog. The three-year-old will also have an awareness that there can be good and bad in the same person, and even the same deeds – the person is sometimes good, sometimes bad. To the three-year-old's way of thinking, punishment can be more aggressive and violent. Sometimes the child's view of punishment is primitive, with death or debilitating injury for fighting, biting or disobeying. At this age, for a child, death is not permanent.

The four-year-old continues to see the possibility of good and bad in the same character, and to cope with the idea that good qualities may exist in what may seemingly be bad characters. A gorilla saves the people. The four-year-old sees the possibility of learning from punishment: the boy was playing with matches and the house burned down. There seems to be a growing concern for the larger social aspects of goodness and badness. Ambulances, fire engines, and police can be seen as the results of misbehavior such as stealing, setting fires, etc.

Children aged five to seven understand more about social responsibility. They understand that acts will have a result. Lying and stealing are ethical social problems, not just personal. There is more concern with immediate results to actions such as mistreating a younger sibling or a pet. Girls at this age seem more concerned with moral personality than the boys as the girls begin to identify with the mother figure and domestic morality. The girl will often try to mete out punishment for what she considers naughty behavior.

Children after the age of seven regard morality and following the rules as the result of agreement among contemporaries, and accept the idea that rules can be changed by means of a democratically arrived at consensus (Piaget & Inhelder, 2000). In other words, before the age of seven children follow the rules because their parents tell them to. After the age of seven, children rely on their own conscience—they know what is right and wrong because they understand the concept of cause and effect.

<u>Being chased/attacked.</u> Being chased sometimes can be traced back to waking situations in which the dreamer felt caught or vulnerable, acted passively, or in which the dreamer "gave in". Being chased by animals or demons can represent the dreamer's own unexpressed or unacknowledged anger or aggression, which is being projected onto the chaser. The pursuer may actually be an unconscious or rejected aspect of the dreamer that is trying to make contact with, or be recognized by, waking consciousness, and may become more frightening if the dreamer resists its efforts (Thomson, 1994).

Children who have dreams of being chased could mean that circumstances are closing in on them. It may also symbolize that emotions are about to be out of control. There may be feelings of getting caught for some deed or action. For some children this may be a sign that they are being bullied at school. Being chased reflects feelings of insecurity. The dreamer is running away from something. The figure who pursues the dreamer represents an unresolved aspect of the dreamer's life (Hamilton-Parker, 1999).

According to research done by Robert Van de Castle (1994), the two most frequent types of dreams are those in which the dreamer is being pursued or attacked and dreams of falling. He found that both males and females typically dreamed of an unprovoked attack by a man or group of men, to which the dreamer responded by fleeing, waking up, or some other escapist action. It is rare that the dreamer will actually fight back. The dream of being attacked could represent the dreamer's self-conception as a weak, passive, inferior, or helpless person at the time the dream appeared.

These types of dreams may represent anxieties concerning the harmful intentions of others towards the dreamer, but in some cases the person in the attacking role represents a projected and disowned part of the dreamer's personality. If a person has had several dreams of this type it could be helpful to ask whether someone has been unusually critical towards him recently. If nobody fits this description it could be an internal action. The dreamer may be acting in a self-saboteur role. There may be an unconscious message being sent saying the dreamer is not adequate or not entitled. If the dreamer continually dreams about being chased by an authority figure, it could be about someone the dreamer is in conflict with (always fighting with Mother, etc.).

Spurr (1999) gives the following dream example of a nine-year-old boy who was being subjected to bullying at school:

"I was racing through our garden as plants lashed out at my ankles. I tried to go faster and faster but they grew longer. One wrapped around my leg, but I managed to keep pulling myself along. I knew they were out to get me. My heart was pounding, and I felt I was going to die if I didn't get out of the garden. As I finally reached the bottom of the garden, our wooden gate became the school gate. It was made of glistening metal and grew taller and taller so I couldn't reach the latch" (p. 82).

Falling. In falling dreams, the height from which a dreamer falls can vary considerably: from falling from the moon to falling into a pit. Several explanations have been offered to account for falling dreams. Downward motion, says Van de Castle (1994), is considered to have negative connotations: Hell is down below and we'll descend to there if we are sinful; we "fall down" on the job if we fail in our work performance; we "land" in the gutter if we don't behave correctly. In a falling dream we no longer have our feet "on the ground," we have "lost our balance," and there is generally nothing we can do in the dream to control our rapid descent or alter our expected demise.

Falling dreams are generally considered to represent situations in which the dreamer feels in danger of losing status, respect, security, or emotional security. An abrupt awakening from the dream just before hitting the ground usually terminates falling dreams. Some people have developed the ability to decelerate their fall so that they float slowly downward or hover in space. By discovering ways to take greater control of waking life and improving self-confidence, falling dreams can be diminished in frequency (Thomson, 1994).

A similar theme is having a dream where the child is stuck in a high place (such as a tree) with no knowledge of how he got there. It may mean that the child is trying to live up to someone's high expectations, either his own or his parents. The child may feel that these expectations are too high. Parental expectations are especially hard to live up to (Wiseman, 1989).

Children, like adults, are susceptible to falling dreams when they feel off balance or out of control. Falling dreams occur most often when there is a sense of chaos in the schedule, when small things mount up or when stability feels somehow shaky. In a few instances, falling dreams may be associated with ear infections or with an injury to the eardrum. If there is no physical element contributing to the falling dream, then it is possible the child is dealing with a sense of slipping, as if the normal taken-for-granted aspects of life may not be holding up somehow. This is a time to reassure the child of the stable elements in her life and to discuss things that may be scary or unsettling to her (Holloway, 2001).

Flying. The contrast to the falling dream is the flying dream. Just as downward movement carries negative associations, upward movement conveys positive associations. We "go up" to Heaven, we "climb" the ladder of success. In many cases, dreams of flying reflect some aspect of the mental self breaking free of the physical self (Eigen, 1981). Various postures may be used in flying dreams: Superman style with arms straight ahead; airplane style with arms at right angles to the dreamer's body; flapping of the arms like bird's wings, or hands on the hips. Swooping through the air with delight shows a great sense of playfulness (Spurr, 1999).

The emotions associated with flying in dreams are usually positive and exhilarating. Many people say the "high" they receive from a flying dream may last for several days. The satisfaction accompanying the sensation of flying is derived from the feeling of having complete control of one's own actions, changing one's direction at will, and encountering no roadblocks. The sky is, literally, the limit while flying. Flying also affords the dreamer a new perspective on situations that might not be easy to view from a lower level. Individuals who enjoy "being on top" experience flying dreams more often than those who have a hard time "getting off the ground" in their everyday activities (Van de Castle, 1994).

A flying dream in which the dreamer is able to achieve only a limited elevation or a brief flight, or encounters obstacles such as power lines, would suggest that the dreamer's aspiration level in some waking task exceeds his current ability. Flying could be an inability to get a grip on something. Flying could also represent a false sense of inflation; acting in a manner not true to self; or not being grounded. If the dreamer actually flies into something, then there may be some worry about obstacles (Holloway, 2001). If the dreamer feels anxiety or fear, he may feel unsupported in some aspect of waking life. For example, if he was flying fearfully over his school there may be something unsettling there.

If the child is flying without fear, usually it means that she feels carefree and happy with her present circumstances, literally flying through life. This type of flying dream allows the child to perform heroic feats by virtue of her magical powers. She can often fly, perform rescues, travel into other realms and generally know what to do to make matters right. These fantasy dreams allow the child to experience success by applying personal powers like imagination, compassion, courage and shrewdness to problem solving.

Children love flying in their dreams and often will fly on magic carpets, in flying ships, with superheroes, or even with the birds (Garfield, 1984). Garfield gives the following dream example of a ten-year-old girl who actually becomes the bird: "I dreamt I am a bird, a beautiful white egret flying in the clouds, and all these bluebirds are around. My feathers blow in the wind as I fly" (p. 263).

Not all flying dreams are for pure pleasure. A common theme among children age six and up is being able to run extremely fast when being chased by bad guys. In the dream, the child sometimes runs so fast and so well that she actually takes off from the ground and begins to fly. The villains give chase, but the child's ability to fly is her safety valve, and she can always outwit the bad guys with this superior power and manage to escape. This tends to be a recurring dream, and it may repeat occasionally, well into young adulthood. Children who have this dream usually have a significant challenge that disturbs them. The villains represent the pressure, and the ability to fly represents their own wish to escape, as well as their own sense that they have the intelligence, imagination and power to make their life work out better. Children who have lost a parent, who face economic struggles, who have a sibling that requires special care or who face some challenge that is part of daily life seem to have this dream (Holloway, 2001).

<u>Getting lost/losing something.</u> This is a dream about finding the way through a situation that seems unfamiliar and insecure. If the dreamer has lost his way, it may suggest losing direction in his life or that the dreamer has lost sight of his goals. Without plans or goals, the dreamer may be feeling insecure. Or perhaps the dreamer is still trying to find the way in a waking situation or one in which the rules or conditions are changing. Dreams about being lost, frequently symbolize the ending of one phase of life and the beginning of the next phase, creating anxiety about leaving behind the familiar. Whatever the situation is, only the dreamer can determine and resolve.

Hartmann (1998) describes how stress can cause dreams of being lost. Some of the common dream images include: "I am in a boat being tossed around on the sea." "I am lost." "I am wandering through buildings and can never find where I am going." "I am walking around (or driving) in a desolate area; I can't find my way; there's no one to help me." Clearly such dreams at times of stress show feelings of vulnerability, of confusion, of feeling lost or hurt. Dreams of being lost often follow traumatic change in the dreamer's waking life. They may also mirror a sense of loneliness.

The things we value the most often serve as an extension of our self-awareness. A favorite hat, car, or relationship reflects a part of how we feel about ourselves. Therefore, the loss of such an object in a dream is significant. It is equally significant whether we actually own the object or not in waking life. If the lost item is an inanimate object, what does it symbolize? For example, losing a wallet may be a sign of a loss of identity in some aspect of the dreamer's life. Loss of jewelry, favored clothes, or pictures and family heirlooms may indicate that the dreamer is nervous about losing an important object in waking life. If a person is lost it could represent the commitment in the relationship the dreamer has with that person. However, it is not unusual to be looking for a stranger. Why is the dreamer searching for this person ? (Lohff, 2000)

A similar theme is the sense of abandonment. Children often express in dreams of being lost their sense of feeling lost in life, of being abandoned. This often occurs after a child's parents divorce. There may be a sense of isolation from the family and of being emotionally neglected by someone. There may also be dreams of abandonment after the death of a loved one. Not only does this issue come up with divorce and death. Most every child has abandonment issues of some degree. Children's fears of being abandoned take many forms: some dream of being kidnapped; others dream that their parents disappear. These dreams often appear in the form of recurring nightmares. When they do, it is a clear indication that the child is undergoing some type of distress (Garfield, 1984).

Garfield gives the following dream example of a five-year-old girl whose parents were divorced and her mother was about to remarry: "I was in a rocker and Mommy was holding me. Then Mommy disappeared. I went looking for her in the street. Some school friends helped me look. We looked in a neighborhood shop. Then a giant-sized woman came along and said, 'Don't worry. I'll hold you.' And she did" (p. 178).

On the other hand, dreams of abandonment may also be a necessary preliminary to being independent. Abandonment may occur in the dreams of young people who are about to go out on their own. It may also represent a need for guidance on some life issue.

<u>Anger.</u> Hall and Van de Castle (1966) found that feelings of anger and fear are twice as common as joy and happiness in dreams. We may find the unresolved events and feelings of waking life expressing themselves in dreams at night. Most contemporary dream analysts believe that one of the functions of dreaming is to allow us to feel and express intense emotion. Since anger is a feeling many of us are uncomfortable expressing while awake, dreams can serve a compensatory function of allowing us to get it off our chests. The particular details of the dream will signal the dreamer to exactly which area of life is being addressed.

We are often very surprised to find ourselves angry in a dream, but dreams may be the first clue that we are expressing feelings of irritation, anger and hurt. Anger dreams can be very refreshing. They can also be very painful. Dreams provide us with a forum for expressing our feelings fully. Sometimes we take advantage of this opportunity by telling off whoever we are angry at. We can let them know how angry and hurt we are, and how we won't put up with it any more. It's amazing how eloquent we can be in our sleep. Such a dream is very refreshing, and there will be a sense of relief.

At times, however, this expression of anger is tied to a great deal of pain. In some dreams, anger is just the first layer, and underneath it lies buried hurt. We can get to that hurt in dreams sometimes by telling someone off, by being angry, and by saying what we are angry about in the waking state. Then we may end the dream by feeling sad because the very thing that made us so angry also hurt our feelings (Delaney, 1997).

Five-year-old Jimmy had just started kindergarten. He discovered that his little brother, Marty, was playing with his toys while he was gone. He dreamed that he came home from school and found Marty sitting in his room surrounded by broken toys. He was so angry that he started yelling at his brother saying, "Get out! I hate you!" After awakening from the dream, Jimmy was still angry and yelled at his mother not to let his little brother in his room while he was at school.

<u>Embarrassment.</u> There are many different topics contained in embarrassing dreams. Sometimes the embarrassment will continue after the dream, carrying it over into waking life. Teeth falling out and being naked in public are the two most common embarrassment dreams.

In a dream about teeth falling out, the person is often afraid someone will see the missing teeth. This could represent "losing face." The dreamer should look at her waking life and see if there is a situation that is similar. There is a saying, "loose lips sink ships," and sometimes the loss of teeth in a dream means that the dreamer is saying things that shouldn't be said. After such a dream, the dreamer can think back and see if there was any negative words being said about someone or something. The dream may be saying to watch what is coming out of the mouth.

Researchers say that people who have recurring dreams of losing their teeth are often more anxious and tend to worry and be upset about things. They have lower self-esteem, tend to be more critical of themselves, and feel more helpless in dealing with life's events (Van de Castle, 1994).

Gillian Holloway (2001) believes that dreams of teeth crumbling, falling out, and leaving a bloody mess represents the cost of making a compromise. People who have this dream are making reasonable choices in situations where their options are limited or forced. Teenagers often have this type of dream. Holloway says these may be the years when people feel the most pressure to compromise for various reasons but haven't yet established enough power to permit greater freedom. The dream doesn't necessarily mean that a mistake has been made, but it points out that a deep and highly personal cost is involved in making the decision.

Appearing nude or inappropriately dressed in public is another subject of embarrassment in dreams. This could represent the dreamer's concern about what others would think if they could see the dreamer as she really is. A child who dreams of nudity may be feeling insecure about something in waking life. The dreamer may also feel exposed or vulnerable, or someone may be making her feel under attack. It may refer to anxiety about revealing intimate details. Nudity may also refer to the uncovering of something that was intended to be hidden.

Dreams of being nude in public are not very common for children. These dreams are usually transitory. If a child has a nudity dream, it is possible to trace the source in some waking situation that caused embarrassment. Eight-year-old Missy had a dream in which she was at the mall wearing transparent pajamas. Feeling embarrassed and ashamed, she noticed that standing nearby was her friend Karen. Waking up, Missy still felt ashamed and thought about how she had recently been confronted by Karen, because she had been gossiping about her to other friends.

A common element to the nudity dream is that no one seems to notice (or care) that the dreamer is nude. This could symbolize that the dreamer should get rid of any feelings or fears of being rejected if the true self is revealed. Holloway (2001) believes this type of dream is usually associated with a sense of unfamiliar exposure due to a change in circumstances. These dreams usually start in adolescence when the dreamer first becomes aware of a social identity and attempts to manage the impressions made on others. Also any problem that puts the dreamer on the spot can cause this type of dream.

Being naked without embarrassment could mean that the dreamer feels comfortable being natural, being herself. Or it could mean that an old role is being shed (represented by clothes) for a new one.

Examination dreams. Examination dreams is another frequent typical dream theme. There are many different types of examination dreams. The most common one is that the dreamer is getting ready to take some type of examination and discovering that the questions can't be understood, they have no writing instrument or the instrument won't work, or the allotted time is not enough to finish the examination. Sometimes the dreamer is late for the test or can't find the place where the examination is being held. An examination dream is a common anxiety dream. It may represent something in the dreamer's life that they've failed, or a fear of failure. The dreamer may be in or about to enter, a waking situation in which he will be tested.

According to Garfield (1984) examination dreams originate when the child is first faced with pressure to perform well in school. She gives the following example: "I am taking an examination. The bell has gone off but my answer is not yet complete. I cannot write a word. The time is up. I am crying" (p.200). If a child has a frightening examination dream it can be asked, "what situation is making the child feel as if he is being tested? How does the child feel unprepared?"

Holloway (2001) says that people who have examination dreams are usually high achievers. They also may be self-critical, expect too much of themselves and worry about not living up to their own expectations. These dreams don't warn of impending mistakes, instead they symbolize the dreamer's belief that performance is crucial to achievement and preparation is necessary in order to perform well. This type of dream can be like a barometer of internal pressure. It tells the dreamer when enough is enough.

The term "examination dream" is also used to describe situations in which the dreamer has to deliver a talk and is speechless, is in the cast of a play and can't remember the lines, or in some other way can't perform in public. The common denominator in all these dreams is that the dreamer feels unprepared or deficient in knowledge and fears judgment by authority figures or peers. Examination dreams are most likely to appear when the person is in doubt about her ability to satisfy some task which could result in serious consequences if there is failure.

Symbols

We all have unconscious tendencies that we are completely unaware of operating within us. The unconscious is the oldest and most primitive part of the mind and it's language is disguised in pictures and symbols. Symbols express what thoughts can't think and feelings can't verbalize. They can embrace and express our inner and outer life, our past, present, and future. A picture or symbol contains a whole idea or concept and can act as the eyes of our inner world. When endeavoring to interpret the messages in our dreams, we need to develop and use the functions of emotion and intuition rather than intellect and sensation. It is best to 'feel' into a dream, or understand its meaning in a flash of intuition. Universal meanings of various symbols followed by the dreamer's personal ones should be considered first.

Our dreams are built with symbols because this is the way our subconscious minds record all of our experiences and impressions. If someone mentions your dog, you immediately picture the dog's face, not the word dog. According to Carl Jung, a dream symbol is the best possible representation of a complex fact not yet grasped by consciousness. Symbols are the unconscious mind's attempt to reveal something to us that is often rich, complex, and difficult to grasp with linear terms. Deciphering our dream symbols can let us face the hidden unconscious.

The most important thing to remember about interpreting symbols is to never be narrow-minded. Symbols are very flexible. Sometimes a symbol has a meaning to one person and a different meaning for someone else. For example, if a person is allergic to strawberries, then dreaming of strawberries could be considered a warning (Sechrist, 1968). When you know the context of a dream and the circumstances of the dreamer's life, you can find the correct meaning.

Basic symbols. Basic symbols are used as guides in which to evaluate the dream, not as an interpretation. The dream interprets itself.

Houses. Houses symbolize ourselves. A house is like the human body or protective shell that "houses" our soul on Earth. It is also our dwelling place - what we think about, where our thoughts reside. The action that takes place in our dream house represents the activity in ourselves. If the image of the house feels comfortable then the child usually feels confident within the family. Being lost in a house could symbolize anxiety within the home. Being locked out of the house could indicate that the child feels excluded from the family (Spurr, 1999). No windows on the house could mean that there is something the dreamer doesn't want to see.

Rooms can also represent different socializations or concerns of the family:
- *Living rooms* could represent everyday or current affairs. Something that is going on at that particular time. The qualities of the room can be thought of as potentials and inner resources of the dreamer. Looking at these qualities may indicate adjustments that need to be made in attitudes or the approach to life.
- *Bedrooms* usually represent intimacy, hidden activities, or issues that are unconscious. The bedroom may also mean that the dreamer needs more rest, either physically or mentally.
- *Kitchens* are where the family comes together for sustenance; it's like the emotional heart of the home. When we're trying to sort out feelings, interpersonal relationships or set priorities we may have dreams set in a kitchen. The kitchen is also a room of magic, where we create new dishes out of existing ingredients. Like the alchemy of life we are building, mixing, and healing situations by experimenting with combinations of energy and intention (Holloway, 2001). A dining table could represent a need to pay attention to diet or what the dreamer is feeding the mind.

Likewise, the doors themselves could have meaning. The back door may represent the past. If something (or someone) is coming *in* the back door, it could be an issue of the past that needs resolution. If the image is going *out* of the door, it could be that an issue from the past has been dealt with. Locking the back door may mean that the dreamer wants to avoid an unpleasant situation. The front door would represent the future (something coming into the dreamer's life) or a current event (Milligan, 1997). Doorways can be seen as openings or avenues of personal expression, new opportunities or potential changes. Unwanted changes are often depicted in dreams as unwanted intruders or strangers coming to the door.

Windows can show up in strange places in a dream house and provide unusual views. Usually windows represent points of view, perspectives, and glimpses of insight. Dreaming of a window could help reveal a perspective on current events or a current predicament. If the dreamer is outside, looking in the window, it could represent a view of the self. If the dreamer is inside, looking out the window, it could represent the dreamer's view of the world. If there are no windows, there could be something the dreamer doesn't want to see.

Houses can also symbolize our minds. We can think of our mind as a three-story house. The main floor is the psychological level, our conscious mind. Just as we spend most of our daytime hours on the main floor of our homes, so too do we use the conscious mind when we are awake. Our attention is more on the inhabitants - on relationships. These dreams sometimes tell us about our feelings. A mirror in the house could represent self-examination or how others see us.

The basement or lower level is the biological level, our subconscious mind. This is where we store things away that we no longer use everyday. This is where we keep our memories - every thought, feeling and experience we've ever had. This is the mental part of our higher self, where our natural ESP is stored. Hearing a voice is usually our subconscious talking to us. It is also where we are likely to focus on the mechanics of operation (furnaces, water heater, etc.). These dreams are sometimes messages from our body - that we feel too cold or too hot, etc. This is also the nighttime version of our conscience that whispers to us during the day.

The upstairs or attic is the spiritual level, our superconscious mind. It is here that we have dreams of the future, or messages from God or the creative source. Some believe this is where we detach our souls at night and fly. It is the highest level of thought - our hopes and dreams, and futures. It is the part of our minds when we are the closest to God. It is also that still, small voice within that guides and protects us.

Vehicles. Children's dreams are often full of symbols concerning transportation. Their lives and personalities change rapidly, and transportation often symbolizes a time to move forward. As the driver, the child expresses a self-image of independence and mastery. As a passenger, the child could be playing the part of a passive person who is dependent upon others.

Cars. Cars usually symbolize our physical ego, our physical body, or our life direction. Just as the soul inhabits the body, when we get into a car the car becomes an extension of us. A new car could represent a new way of life. If the vehicle is going out of control or has no brakes it could mean that something in our life is going out of control. A car accident could show conflict or contention in waking life. Losing our car may mean that we have lost track of ourselves or something in our life. Driving from the back seat could mean that we feel we should be in control but are not (Holloway, 2001).

According to Garfield (1984) losing control of a car is one of the images children conjure up in their dreams as they respond to change. Garfield's fourteen-year-old daughter began having nightmares when the family was getting ready to move to a different country. She described one dream: "A crazy lady let go of the steering wheel. I was trying to grab the wheel and save us." (p. 171)

Anxiety can also bring about dream cars. Attention should be paid to the type of car (big, small, convertible, brand-new, etc.) and to the color of the car, which can represent different emotions. Children are almost always the driver of their dream cars. Four-year-old Eric aimed his dream car toward a barbershop, leaped out before impact, and watched the building explode. Having a haircut was a distasteful activity to the boy, and in his dream he set himself at the wheel to eliminate future visits.

If the child never places himself at the steering wheel in dreams of cars, the likelihood is that he feels life is being controlled by other people. If the child sits at the steering wheel in dreams, this indicates greater self-confidence. Movement from dreams of being a passenger to dreams of being the driver is a healthy change in the child's dream life (Garfield, 1984).

Airplanes. An airplane in a dream often refers to spirituality, hopes and ideals, or thoughts and ideas. For a child, flying a plane can represent taking charge of a situation. The responsibility of being a pilot may symbolize a new skill mastered or a problem solved. If the dream is accompanied by anxiety the child may feel he is on a path that is too difficult. For example, three-year-old Danielle was having recurring dreams of a "cuckoo person driving a beelike airplane." Since it was a recurring dream, it suggested an ongoing anxiety (Garfield, 1984).

If the plane crashes or is never able to take off it could mean that things are stalled or grounded. A helicopter could show a stationary condition - no forward or backward action - just hovering in one place; lack of progress.

Trains. A train ride could represent the journey of life. Trains often represent the dreamer's style of thinking and logic and often show the process being made by following a train of thought. Because trains travel along the ground, trains represent a grounded approach that utilizes logic more than leaps of faith (Holloway (2001).

The train could also symbolize motivation and the power of positive thinking as in the classic story *The Little Engine That Could.* The little train in the story is confronted with an impassable mountain and with the rallying cry of, "I think I can. I think I can," the train is able to accomplish the feat. Children's stories have a lot to do with how a child thinks. If this is one story to which the child relates, then it may be incorporated into the dream with the lesson, "believe in yourself."

Boats. Like the train, a boat can represent the journey of life. A boat crossing a body of water could represent that the dreamer is embarking on a new journey either physically or unconsciously, such as a change in consciousness. Water is associated with emotion and feelings. Traveling over smooth water could symbolize that all is well, and the dreamer is enjoying flowing through life. Drifting helplessly in a boat could symbolize a drifting through life without purpose.

If the boat is traveling over troubled waters there could be a conflict in the dreamer's waking life in some relationship or troubles that are coming. Sechrist (1968) gives the following example: A teenage boy dreamed that he looked through a porthole and saw two green monsters rising out of the ocean and lunging at him.

He slammed the porthole shut just in time to save himself from the monsters. The boy was warning himself against two negative qualities in his own nature. The ocean represented his own unconscious; both creatures rose from his inner depths. The larger of the two monsters represented selfishness, the smaller jealousy. The porthole suggested he take a look at himself, and "close out" those monsters.

Dreaming of the boat captain can represent someone who is in charge and accountable for the lives and wellbeing of others. The boat captain could also represent the higher self, authority, or a source of guidance. For a child, the captain could represent his father or some other authority figure.

Children or babies. Children or babies in dreams may symbolize either recently developing attributes or recently acquired facets of the personality. Unlike childhood, which is a changing state, dreams of babies may represent new beginnings, a new relationship, new ideas or a gift of some kind. It could also mean a major change or move. What is the child in the dream doing? Is she sick or does she need help?

Dreaming about a baby could also symbolize someone that will need teaching, guidance and nurturing. For a child, dreaming about a baby could mean that she feels that she needs to be taken care of, or needs guidance.

Rainbows. A rainbow can represent feelings of joy, good fortune, or luck. It's interesting to watch a happy child drawing, painting or just doodling, often there is at least one rainbow in the picture or the picture will be an array of rainbow colors. A beautiful rainbow usually symbolizes the happiness the child feels with life at that moment. A rainbow may also symbolize good news, hope and the end of gloom. The rainbow is a bridge between heaven and earth, between the earthly self and the higher, enlightened self.

Water. Water is a common element in dreams, sometimes threatening, sometimes pleasurable. Water can be seen as the mother of all living organisms, the source of physical creation. It can also be the cleansing force as one moves from one experience to the next. If the water in a dream is crystal clear, it is usually spiritual. Clear water could also represent clear understanding. Moving water is spiritual growth. Muddy water could mean some type of trouble or unclear understanding.

If the dreamer is drowning he should find out why there is fear of the water. He may be literally "drowning" in negative emotions. If the water is being crossed, it could be some type of journey. Water also represents feelings and moods. Tidal waves, backed-up sewers, and leaking basements tend to symbolize an overdose of feelings that can accompany unwanted changes or deep uncertainty. Water in natural settings such as rivers, lakes and oceans tend to represent life situations.

Spurr (1999) says that jumping into the water without fear represents a sense of joy. It resembles the toddlerhood pleasure of stomping in puddles. Sinking in water can indicate anxiety. Does the child feel unable to cope with something? Whirling or being swallowed up by water could represent some fear the child has.

Parts of the body. When a part of the body is emphasized in a dream, it is usually suggesting a specific problem with that area.

Head. The dreamer's head in a dream usually means the functioning of the brain. It can also represent the dreamer's attitudes, way of thinking, or personality. If the dream character's head is on backwards, it could mean things are being approached in a backward fashion. A headless character could be an inability to reach that person through normal or physical ways, therefore only being able to be reached through the consciousness or through spirit. It could also mean that the dreamer is not using his head.

Hair. Hair can symbolize reasoning processes, thought or knowledge. Having a new haircut or having tangled hair can reflect the types of thoughts that are being dealt with. Receiving a shampoo and new hairstyle may mean that it is necessary for a clean, new approach. Trying to comb snarled hair suggests that the dreamer needs to straighten out her thinking.

In the dream of a teenage girl, her boyfriend was busily engaged in disheveling her long hair. She was trying to free herself. The girl later confessed that her boyfriend had been pressuring her to have sex with him by trying to convince her that premarital sex was perfectly acceptable. Despite her moral standards, her boyfriend's arguments were beginning to sound plausible. Her disheveled hair in the dream showed her mental confusion (Sechrist, 1968).

Face. Our face is the portion of the self most often seen by others and most often judged by ourselves. However, the face is more than what we choose to show the world. It is also the intersection between the whole self and the world. For this reason, the face is associated with psychological territory which is highly charged for most people. If we are wearing a mask or heavy makeup in the dream, it could symbolize that we are hiding our real selves from the world, or a fear that something in our life will be exposed. Dreaming of our face, we may find something we find embarrassing or strange that we think should be concealed. This suggests that we are anxious to be liked and that we want to be seen for who we are and not judged on what seems to be a flaw or eccentricity.

Sometimes we judge ourselves in our dreams. The subconscious often uses a disfigurement of the face to dramatize a defect in character. This can be seen by Sechrist's (1968) example of a teenage girl's dream: "I had a blackhead on the side of my face, near the nose. It was as large as an orange! I squeezed it out, and it left a hole near my ear, so that people could see inside my head. I knew I should clean the hole with alcohol. My hair looked dirty" (p. 56).

Sechrist explains that a blackhead, a hole in the head, a nose, and dirty hair all mar the beauty of this teenage girl. In their discussion, the girl admitted she enjoyed hearing (ear) and learning (nosy) about the failings of others and passing this gossip on to others. The large blackhead represented this ugly part of her character. The hole in her head was equated with gossip, for it allowed what is in

25

her head to pass out to others. The dream admonished her to squeeze that black-ness or impurity from herself. The cleansing with alcohol suggested the urgency for her to be clean and antiseptic so that she would no longer infect others with gossip; for people were already seeing through her (hole in her head). She promised she would turn over a new leaf and clean up her thinking (hair).

Special emphasis on the facial features and expressions of people in the dreams enhances their significance. For instance, a large mouth usually symbolizes, "You talk too much." If the dream character has unusually sharp teeth, it could represent sharp words being spoken by that someone in waking life. Likewise, if the person has infected teeth, it could mean that the person has been talking about the dreamer (Sechrist, 1968).

Hands. Doing things with their hands frequently occurs in children's dreams, perhaps because so much learning and creative work involves their hands. Things slipping through the hands generally means that the child is fearful of something. Trying to grasp with the hands reveals the motivation to accomplish a particular task or skill. Twisting the hands may show that the child is anxious about something that is happening in waking life. Cupping something with the hands indicates that the child is treasuring something. Whatever is being cupped may represent feelings, an object, an actual person, or pet (Spurr, 1999).

Hands can also represent our ability to grasp and control our destiny. We can think of our hands as representing the authority we have over our own life. Hands could also represent creativity; we make things with our hands. Dreams of losing a hand or having it damaged can symbolize a warning that the sense of authority or creative freedom is being threatened in some way. A huge hand, especially coming from the sky could mean the hand of God. Fingers are associated with our individual personality and our freedom to express ourselves in many ways. Shaking hands with someone shows friendship.

Legs. Legs in a dream can symbolize things such as personal balance, stability or direction. Usually, one meaning of dreaming about the left side can correspond to the past and the right side can correspond to the future. Also the wrong (left side) way and the right (right side) way. Legs are often a symbol of relationships. If something happens to a leg it could mean there is some type of conflict in a waking relationship. For example: losing a leg may represent that a relationship is over. Being legless in the dream may show a poor foundation in efforts to deal with a current problem or activity. Seeing another person legless may show poor insight into what the other person represents.

Feet. Feet are the pathway that we are on and our ability to move forward. Feet represent our foundation in life, the assumptions upon which we build our existence, and the principles we use to make decisions and move forward. It could also mean that the dreamer is grounded or down to earth with thoughts and actions. Dreaming of feet may reflect issues with the family. Shoes on the feet often reflect the role we are using as we stride through life. Being barefoot may indicate a sense of freedom or naturalness. Bare feet can also represent vulnerability. When it is painful or difficult being barefoot, it could mean there are feelings of being ill equipped (Holloway, 2001).

Structures. A bridge is our way of passing through material life, or a transition between two periods of our life. It could also represent a crossing using the conscious mind, in contrast with a way through the unconscious, which could be signified by a tunnel. While a bridge may represent the support in our life, a broken bridge would symbolize loss of support.

A wall may symbolize an obstacle that needs to be overcome. Alternatively, we may be "up against a wall" where some type of action must be taken. Likewise, a fence may represent some type of barrier. A fence could also mean that we are confining ourselves in some way, either consciously or unconsciously, such as by attitude. Someone else's actions may be restricting us in some way. We may be undecided about something, "on the fence."

People. Friends and family members are often used as symbols. Sometimes they represent the dreamer and sometimes they represent another friend or family member; and sometimes they represent themselves. When familiar people are in the children's dreams, it is important to check the emotions that accompany the image. The thing that irritates us the most about other people is found in the self. We don't like to admit bad qualities in ourselves so we "project" them onto someone else.

A person's behavior in a dream could indicate the dreamer's behavior. For example, a girl had a recurring dream that consisted of people she knew well, adults as well as children, appearing to her as tiny people. They were so small she could easily have held them in the palm of her hand, yet they were going about their daily tasks in a normal manner. The dream symbolized that her "other self" was trying to impress her with her own value, for she was a very timid child. She was being urged to express herself with greater confidence and courage (Sechrist, 1968).

The person in the dream may have been selected just because of their name. The person may represent somebody with the same name. For example, if someone in the dream is named John, it could represent someone the dreamer knows who is also named John. The name itself may have a meaning, such as someone named Art could represent a need for creativity.

Dreaming of a person can also refer to that person's job or career. For example, dreaming of someone who is a teacher could symbolize school. Likewise, dreaming of school could represent the teacher. Another meaning is that the dream could represent the dreamed of person's qualities. Dreaming of a girl who is intelligent, gracious, and patient may symbolize a need for the dreamer to mirror those qualities.

Parents. According to studies done by Foulkes (1982), once children reach the age of five parents are dreamed of more often by children who are passive and whose family situations seems less than optimal. Parent irritability will often predict the children's dreaming of them. A child that is having a conflict with a parent will more than likely have a dream involving that parent.

Because of the changing relationship between parents and children an unpleasant parent image may simply reflect a transitory problem, although it could indicate a longer-term difficulty. If the parent image is looming, the child could be feeling intimidated or may feel the parent is being too strict or harsh. If the parent is seen as a shadow the child may be feeling emotionally abandoned. Dreaming that a frightening man is standing at the end of the bed could symbolize feelings of guilt about parental discord (Spurr, 1999).

The demons of children's dreams are often - although not always - the parents transformed. It is difficult to see a parent in a cruel way, so the child turns the parent into a nightmare image. For example, Jimmy dreamed about a monster that was being mean to him. In waking life, Jimmy believed that his father was being mean by making him do his homework instead of letting him play with his friends. The dream monster had become a substitute for his father. In this way, the pain, and perhaps anger, is directed towards the dream image instead of the offending parent (Garfield, 1984).

Friends. Children's dreams may reflect the emotional nature of their close friendships. If the friend is seen as an equal, it will show the child's happiness with the friendship. If the friend is hiding in the dream, it could mean that the child is feeling isolated or lonely. A friend that is seen in the background may be the dreamer herself. If the child is being taunted in the dream, she may have experienced some bullying in waking life or is feeling insecure with her friends.

Sometimes the situation surrounding the friend in the dream will reveal something about the dreamer. The dreamer may be experiencing something similar to what the friend is experiencing in waking life, or perhaps the friend has the same looks, traits or personality as the dreamer. Then the dreamed of friend could represent the dreamer. Children may dream of their peer group at school in the same way as they dream about their friends (Spurr, 1999).

Relatives. Dreams that include relatives may give an idea about how the child feels about the extended family. This may be more or less important, depending on the family's circumstances. For example, if there has recently been a divorce or some other conflict, then support from relatives would be desired. How does the child interact with the relatives in the dream? How do the relatives in the dream act towards the child?

Dreaming of grandparents could represent wisdom or spiritual inheritance. The relationship with grandparents in waking life could determine the meaning of the dreams. Does the child have a fun, loving relationship, a strained relationship or even a nonexistent relationship? Grandparents are usually seen by children to be more sympathetic than parents. Parents have to be obeyed, but a grandparent's advice is usually listened to and voluntarily applied (Hamilton-Parker, 1999).

Strangers. According to Sylvia Browne (2002), research has shown that children don't tend to include strangers in their dreams until around the age of six. Before that age, they usually only dream of people in their own familiar immediate vicinity.

A stranger could represent an authority figure. Sometimes a stranger in a frightening dream may represent a real person that the child is having difficulty with or is afraid of. Alternatively, the stranger may symbolize unpleasant feelings the child is having. Strangers asking questions is an uncomfortable image that may represent something that is being asked of the child, either at home or school. Being under observation or questioned by strangers, usually relates to anxiety of some sort. If the stranger is joining in the activities of the dream, the child may be feeling lonely and adds new people to keep them company (Spurr, 1999).

Famous People/Being Important. Dreaming of famous people such as rock stars and sports figures may mean that the child wants to emulate them as role models. Celebrities are usually symbols of the quality or activity for which they are known. Just as generic dream characters are stereotypes of personality traits, celebrities are often shorthand symbols for outstanding talents and attributes. The meaning of the celebrity may be a combination of what the dreamer most identifies with them and their overall public persona. The child may aspire to achieve what the famous person has or reflect a talent and resources the dreamer already has. The child may just create a fantastical dream where they are a part of the dream image's group, such as rockin' with a rock band (Holloway, 2001).

According to Garfield (1984), when children visualize themselves as important without describing the behavior involved in achieving this status, they may not yet realize how to achieve goals in life. If the child reports such dreams, parents should show that they understand the desire by comments like "How did that feel? That must have been fun. It sounds like a great adventure." Aside from wanting to be a famous person, children also bestow importance on themselves in dreams by becoming royalty. The role of princess is particularly popular with girls. Five-year-old Aaron dreamed his mother was a princess and he a prince.

Cartoon Figures. Using images from cartoons probably provide suitable material for expression that the child can't otherwise visualize because of their age or cognitive ability. It could also mean that someone in waking life is acting out like a cartoon character, such as dreaming about Goofy.

Super Heroes. According to Garfield (1984), the superhero or superheroine represents a deep need children have for more control of their lives. Perhaps because boys and girls are so much smaller and less powerful than the adults around them, tales of the superhero have always been popular. Children yearn for a powerful figure on whom they can pin their hopes for overcoming difficulties. Such figures help children evolve their own mastery.

Figures who can accomplish the impossible are very useful for children at a certain stage of development. They provide a fantasy character on whom they can focus their daydreams as well as their night dreams. If a child's obsession with superheroes endures into adolescence, however, and fictional heroes and heroines are not gradually replaced by living men and women who have managed to make contributions of value, the child is left adrift in a sea of fantasy.

The superhero figures of our mass media tend to overemphasize physical power, even violence, in accomplishing their feats of heroism. Parents can add to their child's supply of heroes and heroines by sharing stories, legends, and films that portray a variety of outstanding people, fictional and real, with a range of skills beyond superhuman strength. If a child has frequent dreams about being a superhero, chances are the child is reaching for strength, achievement, importance, and self-reliance.

Animals. Animals in dreams may symbolize instincts that the child may identify with or they can be symbolic parts of the child's self, talents, abilities, personality or even flaws. Animals may represent other people the child knows. If the animal is talking in the dream it could mean that something or someone is trying to get the child's attention. Determining what the animal represents will show the child what the message is.

Certain animals are extremely prevalent in dreams and have universal associations. We must look at the nature of the animal as it is presented and notice the child's feelings toward it and feelings for it. In this way, the image of the animal and her reaction to it is considered together to find the meaning of the dream. It's important to know that all animal symbols have positive and negative potentials. The interpretation of the animal depends on the aspect of the dream.

When the animals in our dreams are presented in their negative potential, we're alerted to the nature of a threat we're dealing with in waking life and gain a sense on how to deal with the situation. When animals need our help or appear in their positive potential, we can learn a lesson about our deepest nature or about an essential need. Gillian Holloway (2001) says there are a few rules about getting the most from our animal dreams:

- Hostile, threatening animals tend to represent a troubling person or problem in the child's life.
- Dream animals in need of rescue or care almost invariably represent a part of the child that she feels has been neglected or abandoned.

Family Pets. Family pets in children's dreams tend to represent security. Frequently, the dream consists of an adventure in which the pet is included. If the child is feeling unsure of something, the pet may be pushed forward (Spurr, 1999). If, on the other hand, the pet is attacking the child or is in some way being aggressive, the child may be expressing some type of conflict or fear in waking life. If the child is being aggressive towards the pet in the dream, it could symbolize anger or hostility the child is feeling.

If the pet's behavior is emphasized or unusual things happen to it, then the symbolic image should be explored more. For example, if the pet is sick or dies in the dream it could be a warning to take better care of the animal. The dream could also be suggesting that the child should take better care of herself (Garfield, 1984).

Snakes. The snake is one of the world's oldest symbols. Ask people what they think of snakes and many of them will tell you that they are afraid, very afraid of snakes. For some people it is an irrational, devastating fear. For this type of person, a snake in a dream will represent fear. But not everyone is afraid of snakes and many people actually love them. To this type of person, dreaming of a snake is a positive dream. Snakes can symbolize many different things. Looking at the nature and traits of the individual breed of snake can also determine the meaning.

For the positive potential, some snakes are associated with initiations of power in the psyche. They appear as a single snake that has to be passed by in order to proceed or you have to befriend the snake despite your fear. In some dreams, snakes are associated with the boundary between life and death, matter and spirit, past and future. Snakes may represent healing, as it is the symbol on the medical profession's caduceus. A snake in a coiled position could represent a spiral, a spiral which is indicative of rising energy, from smaller to larger. It would symbolize the higher consciousness of the self, springing forward (Scallion, 1997). The snake is also a symbol of transformation because the skin is shed on a regular basis.

The negative potential of snakes, especially for children, can often represent a problem or troublesome situations that are intimidating and disturbing. This is most common if the dream consists of a pit of snakes or piles of snakes on the floor. A snake image may symbolize a fear in waking life that needs to be dealt with or a hidden fear. Some people believe that the snake represents the dark side or evil. Snakes can also represent deception, such as a "snake in the grass."

Dogs. Dogs are the most popular animal in children's dreams. They are someone who can be either faithful or unfaithful. Dogs are usually considered to be man's best friend, but if aroused, the dog becomes an enemy. A dog as a family pet is usually very loyal. On the other hand, a strange dog is not always to be trusted. If you run they will chase. Just as in waking life, the dog in a dream can alert the dreamer to some type of danger by barking or some other behavior.

The positive potential of a dog is that they are associated with love and loyalty. If the child dreams of a dog that is hurt or injured, it could be a part of the child's own nature that needs healing. A dog in need can represent that the dreamer needs to be loyal to herself or to get her out of a situation that is hurting her. If the dog's tail is wagging it can symbolize a happy and fun dream.

The negative potential of dogs are the cases of wild or mean dogs that are threatening. These dreams may represent a situation that is troubling for the child or someone close to her. She may feel vulnerable or helpless. If the dog is straining on his leash, it could symbolize the child's own anger that needs to be expressed. If the dog's tail is tucked between the back legs, it could represent guilt or shame.

Horses. Horses are another common animal dream symbol. The positive potential of the horse is that they can represent a child's yearning for adventure. The child may be ready for new activities. Horses often symbolize the spirited side of the self that may be in need of stimulation or movement. The horse also symbolizes physical power.

The negative potential of the horse is that it may reflect the body's vitality. If the horse in the dream is exhausted or injured, it could mean that the dreamer has become a workhorse and in need of either physical or mental rest (Foulkes, 1967). Horses often have quick starts, but they also panic easily. Looking at the color of the horse may help discover the meaning of the dream.

Alligators. Positive potential alligator dreams are rare but they can signal that a problem has come up that needs immediate attention. They may symbolize a need for some type of healing. The alligator may also be a signal to take a new perspective on something. Alligators are slow moving then suddenly move with incredible speed, often becoming vicious. When an alligator grabs onto something there is no letting go. If this occurs in the dream, it may be showing the dreamer's tenacity in dealing with some situation in waking life.

The negative potential of an alligator dream usually represents problematic situations that are intense but usually not of long duration. The alligator can be a symbol of aggressiveness. An alligator can also symbolize anger - either the dreamer's or someone else's anger directed at the dreamer (Garfield, 1984). The alligator may also represent hidden instincts, which may feel potentially dangerous and destructive.

Elephants. The positive potential for elephants is their uncanny long memories. Elephants in dreams may be a need to remember something or to make sure something is not forgotten. Elephants also represent enormous power and might. This strength may be connected to the dreamer's intentions and motivations. The elephant may also represent the self's inner strength and wisdom. Elephants fear nothing. For a child, the elephant may represent someone who is strong and can take care of them.

Negative dreams about elephants are rare, but if the elephant is stampeding, it could signal the child's anger. When elephants in the wild become enraged, they will go on a rampage and run over and crush everything in their path. This could be a warning for the child to control his anger in waking life.

Wild Animals. According to Gillian Holloway (2001), children will dream of wild animals more often after they begin school. Lions and tigers are particularly common in younger children's dreams. Older children often dream of wolves, panthers, gorillas, bears or other exotic animals. Wild animals tend to become linked to a particular person with whom the child may be having trouble, or a troubling situation.

Wild animals frequently appear in nightmares, representing some type of fear or anxiety in the child. Wild animals can also symbolize danger, either from the dreamer's unconscious or from some other person. Exploring how the child feels about the animal can help discover what is being symbolized.

Here are a few examples of wild animals and their positive/negative potentials.

- **Lion** energy is valiant and courageous. It moves against the odds and carries one forward into victory. A lion often symbolizes personal power. A lion can also symbolize aggression or anger by the dreamer or some other person.
- **Wolves** symbolize loyalty to the passion of life; the vital part of the psyche that needs freedom, solitude and authenticity. Wolves that are frightening often symbolize a devouring tendency or something that is out of control, such as in the story of Little Red Riding Hood. They may represent a "sheep in wolf's clothing."
- **Bears** often symbolize an inner force and strength that is ready to be tapped. Bears can be very playful. They can also be very destructive. Bears that menace or chase in a dream can represent a man with dominating or frightening characteristics.

Birds. Dreaming of birds may symbolize a desire to move on; or flight without fear. The child may literally fly away with the bird. A bird could also be delivering a message, either good or bad. In mythology, birds are messengers from the gods. Birds may also represent spirituality, showing wholeness, balance and healing (Hamilton-Parker, 1999). Exploring the child's emotions during and after the dream should determine what the bird represents.

According to Sechrist (1968), dreams of birds come when we go through critical periods in our lives. Many teenagers when entering puberty will dream of an eagle pecking or tearing at their heart. This often represents the emotional entanglements that they are subject to and incapable of understanding. These entanglements usually relate to the awakening of their physical bodies at puberty and at the same time the desire to love and be loved without always understanding the responsibilities that mature love demands.

Birds are generally thought of as gentle creatures, soft and sensitive with the special ability to being able to fly. The type of bird, the bird's activity and the dreamer's association with the bird are the key to the meaning. For example, birds of prey will have a different meaning then a tamed parakeet. Flying feathers could represent confusion. Whenever a bird appears in the child's dream, observe carefully the role it plays - attacker, friendly part of nature, or spirit like companion of flight. Each aspect speaks to an emotion taking place within the child at the moment (Garfield, 1984).

Here are a few examples of birds and their positive/negative potentials.

Parrots are birds of great intelligence, sensitivity and devotion. They represent a verbal disposition and quick thinking. Parrots are also associated with repeating everything they've seen or heard. The parrot (as in all symbols) may represent the dreamer or someone else. The child may be parroting something from waking life.

Eagles represent freedom, power, and spiritual energy. Eagles are also symbolic of strategic intellect and the ability to make wise decisions. On the other hand, eagles are devourers of small animals, shredding their prey to pieces.

Owls are often symbolic of great wisdom and unusual powers of discernment. The owl's keen eyesight makes them symbolic of great perception and the ability to decipher mysteries. Owls sometimes appear in a dream as symbols to a passing era, the passing of a loved one or a metaphorical death of some kind. They are not predictors of death but may represent the ending of something or letting go.

Insects. Dreaming of insects usually symbolizes an irritation of some type. They can assume frightening proportions in dreams where the child may feel suffocated by their presence. If this occurs, the parent should find out what is overwhelming the child during waking life. If a dream consists of an eight-legged creature that reaches out and grabs the child and won't let go, the child may feel unable to escape an unpleasant situation. According to Delaney (1997) insects may represent siblings.

Children are prone to dreaming about insects in their bed or a swarm of bugs coming into their room at night when they are facing unpredictable situations, such as a separation in their parent's marriage, moving into a new home, or a new sibling being brought home. According to Holloway (2001), there is no single catalyst or interpretation for the attacking insects; rather, the frightening dream seems to reflect a sense of bewilderment and being overwhelmed. Arguments, unexpected changes, and feeling as if she has no control over events may trigger repetitions of the dream.

However, there can be good potential in an insect dream image. Insects may symbolize the power of small things to create large results. They represent paying attention to the small details of getting a job done.

Here are a few examples of insects and their positive/negative potentials.

Spiders symbolize creativity and the weaving of something successfully. Spiders also represent patience and success through skill. The downside of spiders is that they represent small things that evoke large fears. Scary spiders in dreams may symbolize current challenges that are evoking personal fears.

Ants represent patience, industry and work. These are testimonies to the power of intention, organization, and persistence. The negative side of ants can be a representation of the robotic work syndrome and boredom.

Bees represent fertility and productive thought processes. On the other hand, bees may symbolize busy thoughts or frantic internal chatter. Words and ideas buzz around in the mind making it hard to think calmly (Holloway, 2001).

Lots of animals and insects have powerful associations for children with songs, nursery rhymes, stories, movies, etc. The associations for the child should be considered when interpreting a symbol. For example, in the story *Charlotte's Web* the spider is a heroine. There are many horse stories such as *Black Beauty* and *National Velvet*. *The Story of Babar*, a classic, is about the adventures of a little elephant. Another childhood favorite is *The Velveteen Rabbit*. Dogs, such as Rin-Tin-Tin and Lassie, have always played a large part in children's lives as being heroes they watch on television.

<u>Colors.</u> Color appears in dreams in many ways. For example, an image may be completely or partly in color (such as a red ball). Certain shapes or areas may be colored (such as white squares or blue backgrounds). Most commonly the total scene or entire dream will be in natural color (such as green grass, blue sky, etc.). Color is a symbol and in dreams colors are like emotional tones, reflecting how the dreamer feels about a certain situation and also what potential it holds for the dreamer. For example, if a person vividly recalls a red dream image, then the dream may have been about anger.

Many people don't pay attention to the colors in their dreams. However, learning about the significance of colors may encourage the dreaming mind to be more conscious of them. Like animals, some colors have universal meanings along with positive and negative potentials. If the colors are clear and beautiful, it's usually a positive symbol; if the colors are dull, or cloudy looking then the meaning will usually be negative.

Black. Since black is often associated with mystery, the positive potential of black in a dream can be an indication of a readiness to explore the unknown or something that had been off-limits before. Black can represent the unconscious. Some cultures believe that black is a spiritual color. It can also represent strength.

The negative potential of black in a dream is that it can represent obstructions. It could also indicate that the issue in question is outside the conscious awareness. It's in the dark still. Dreaming about the situation in black imagery may be a sign that the dreamer is ready to tackle the issue. Black is often associated with depression and death.

According to Garfield (1984), black in children's dreams often represents an unknown evil. The reason for this may be because in our culture black is often used in situations from mourning and funerals to the wearing of black hats by villains. Black for a child could also be connected with feelings of gloom and depression.

Garfield gives the following example of a seven-year-old girl's dream: "I was at home all by myself, and a black car drove up. A man dressed in black came out. He came up to the door. And then the dream ended" (p. 132).

Blue. One of the most common positive potentials of blue is that it symbolizes calm and peacefulness. Blue can also mean the truth, personal will or religious/spiritual feelings. Blue is the major intellectual and mind color. Blue is also the color associated with teaching and speaking your truth. Blue can symbolize harmony and freedom (like the sky). Blue can also bring sleep and lower blood pressure.

The negative potential of blue is that it may symbolize sadness or depression; the person is "feeling blue." There will often be a feeling of sadness in the dream, which will reflect the negative potential.

Gold. The positive potential of gold is that it can mean something valuable, powers of the soul, or truth of mind. A gold fabric could mean truths being shown, or something valuable being uncovered. Gold can also represent money, as in gold coins. Gold can represent spiritual knowledge and walking the golden path. A golden light shining on something may signify that it is the holy way. If an object is gold colored it usually symbolizes that it has good qualities. A golden doorknob could represent a new opportunity (Sechrist, 1968).

The negative potential of gold may be of something being hidden or unattainable if the gold is tarnished. Piles of gold coins could symbolize greed or ill-gotten wealth. Gold can also represent temptation. If the gold object looks cheap, tacky or artificial it may symbolize the phrase "all that glitters is not gold."

Green. The positive potential of green is that it is the color of development, growth and renewal. Green can also represent nature. Dreaming of new plants may indicate future growth for the dreamer. Green often symbolizes healing. Green is the major balancing color and can act as an emotional soother.

The negative potential of green is imagery of green sludge on a stagnant pond or mold on food. This can indicate that growth is stunted or being neglected. Green can also symbolize envy, jealousy, insecurity and greed.

Orange. The positive potential of orange is that it represents vitality and feelings and indicates an ability to identify with the emotions of others. Orange will often show up when the dreamer is making positive life changes and is often associated with balance and healing. As an energy focused color, orange is very stimulating for motivation and mental stimulation. Orange is the color for ideas and mental concepts. Often orange will be seen as something in natural form such as changing leaves, fruit or the sky.

The negative potential of orange is that it can represent strong emotions that have a toxic or draining quality. When orange appears in its negative potential, there is often an uncomfortable quality about it, like a jarring sensation, such as a wrong note in a song or mismatched colors. It may be seen as ugly, tacky or an ill-chosen item.

Red. The positive potential of red is that it symbolizes the desires of the heart. Red also symbolizes life energy, a sense of exhilaration, and excitement. It can indicate a passion for life and is a strong physical and emotional color. Red can also be a symbol of religious and spiritual movements, signifying the fight against evil.

The negative potential of red is that it can represent blood, anger, trouble or misunderstandings. Red can also symbolize battles and war and is an almost universal warning symbol. It could represent a threat to the dreamer's physical well-being. The danger is usually immediate and intense. In this sense, seeing red in a dream doesn't mean that something dire is about to happen, but images in red should be evaluated carefully (Holloway, 2001). There will usually be a sense of dread or danger involved so that the negative potential will be easily recognized.

Red absorbs all colors. In a dream, the person has to absorb everything that is going on. If a child is dreaming in red (red house, red car, and red flowers), it could be an indication that, instead of controlling the situation, the child may feel that it is out of her control. She may feel as though she has no resources to handle a situation in waking life.

White. The positive potential of white is that it is the color of purity and is often used in dreams that symbolize spirituality. White can also symbolize innocence. People will dream of themselves dressed all in white, living in a white house, surrounded by people in white robes and so forth. A white flower or butterfly can represent hope and lightheartedness. White clothes, homes, or animals can indicate an openness and faith that something good is yet to come. White can also symbolize renewal after experiencing some type of tumultuous passage.

The negative potential of white is seeing it as a positive veneer over more complex issues and conditions. This can indicate a denial, or a covering, about the positive potential of white. The dreamer may believe, or wants to believe, that the image is a positive energy, but it's not. In this strained positivism, there will be dream images of white plastic items, white paint, shoe polish, and makeup. If the white items in the dream are tacky looking or artificial, it is time to look at the situation more clearly to see if ulterior motives are involved. White can also symbolize coldness.

Yellow. The positive potential of yellow is that it is associated with sensitivity to feelings and subtle influences. Yellow also represents clarity, the logical mind and reasoning powers. Yellow sunlight, flowers, or a gold beam of light can symbolize a kind of intuitive certainty that a hunch or instinct is right. Yellow is also a communication color and represents mental creativity, thinking and speaking. A round yellow object may represent the sun, which symbolizes strength, energy and the circle of life. If a child dreams of sunny landscapes, she is most likely feeling happy and positive at the moment.

The negative potential of yellow is feeling compelled to behave or feel in certain ways that are not necessarily desirable to the dreamer. If the object in the dream is a striking yellow, and it doesn't suit the occasion or the dreamer's taste, it may be in the negative potential. Yellow is also the color of cowardice and fear. Yellow may symbolize illness, or a fear of illness approaching.

Numbers. Numbers often show up in dreams. Sometimes they can represent the actual number, for example, the number may be the same as someone's address, phone number, age, birthday, and so on. A number that does correspond to something familiar may then be a reference to an actual place (address) or person (birthdate). Numbers in dreams can also represent a period of time, for example, number 3 may represent the third month (March), the 3rd day of the month, 3 days, 3 weeks and so on.

Also to be considered is multiples of a particular dream image. For example, a woman dreamed she was in a favorite chair, and there were three cats sitting on her lap. The number three may be significant (along with the cat symbol). Likewise, there may be seven cows or eight trees in a dream, signifying that specific number. To understand the significance of a number, other aspects of the dream needs to be considered.

Listed below are some of the basic numbers and their general meanings. As in all symbols, the particular meaning has to be determined by the dreamer. Some people have a certain number that they believe is their lucky number, so that number would have a different meaning for them.

One. One is a new beginning and is the number that initiates action. The number one may represent the source of life or oneness of all creation.

Two. Two can represent duality and the union of opposites, such as yin and yang, male and female, or heaven and earth. Two can also represent cooperation and the ability to make things work, following the action that began with the number one.

Three. The number three is often thought of to be the perfect number. It can represent the union of the body, mind, and spirit. Three can also symbolize the Holy Trinity. Three of anything in a dream could mean some type of movement and change.

Four. Four is often the number of wholeness, stability and harmony. The four may also represent the four seasons or the four mental functions of thought, feeling, sense and intuition. The number four is often considered a lucky number, as in finding a four-leaf clover.

Five. Five may represent the link between the heavens and the earth. Five can also symbolize travel and movement. For some people, the five represents personal will.

Six. Six usually symbolizes inner harmony and perfection. It could also represent love and romance, or compassion. The six could also refer to friendship.

Seven. Seven is often the symbol of completeness. Seven may represent spirit and the mystical side of things, representing the seven spiritual centers of the body. For many people, the number 7 is a lucky number.

Eight. Eight is the number of power, authority, big creations and enterprise. The eight can represent regeneration and new beginnings. It can also symbolize luck and good fortune. It is the number of bearing the fruits of your labor.

Nine. Nine is the number of completion and endings. It can also represent eternity. The number nine can also symbolize a new beginning since after completion comes something new.

Basic Interpretation Methods

The dream cannot be fully understood without knowing something about the life of the dreamer. The most common dream contains more than one scene, which unfolds as the dreamer is carried along, either as an observer or as a participant. In a dream with more than one scene, the first scene usually gives the setting, like a backdrop in a play. It sets the stage of the progressive message of the dream. However, the scene changes can offer a different viewpoint of the same subject or express the same idea in different ways rather than revealing a progressive message (Milligan, 1997). Listed below are some of the most common basic interpretation methods.

<u>Free Association.</u> Sigmund Freud, who believed that dreams are made up of memory traces of past waking life episodes, pioneered free association. According to Freud, these memory traces can come from the preceding day (day residues) or the distant past. Free association involves letting the person talk freely about the dream images, thereby providing information about thoughts, feelings, motives, and so forth. The dreamer gives a running account of whatever comes into the mind about the dream, regardless of how seemingly irrelevant it may seem. Vocalizing all of the thoughts, feelings, and desires that come from the dream leads to others. The reason this method works is the belief that associations are determined by like events.

The purpose of free association is to explore thoroughly the unconscious mind, gaining access to hidden thoughts and fears. Through free association, dreams that hold repressed memories help to bring those memories into the open. For example, the dreamer may be asked to free associate with a dream image such as a bull. The dreamer is then asked what a bull is and what does it mean. The dreamer then gives a series of thoughts or impressions such as, a bull - cow, milk, bottle, baby; or bull pen, baseball, diamond, engagement ring. Thus, free association reveals the dreamer's thought processes. Very young children however, are not very adept at free associating their dreams (Foulkes, 1978).

Amplification. Pioneered by Carl Jung, the amplification approach is focusing on a single dream image. Amplification is a simple way of working with symbols by attempting to expand the dreamer's associations with the symbol. Using the amplification approach, the dreamer is asked to describe the dream image in every detail. One good way of doing this is to tell the dreamer to imagine he is talking to someone from outer space who has no knowledge of what the object is. Then the dreamer describes the object in every way possible. Using the previous bull image, the dreamer may say something such as, a bull is big, a bull is strong, a bull is masculine, a bull has horns, a bull is dangerous, and so forth. Expanding further the dreamer may ask, "What is a bull?" "What do I like or dislike about a bull?" "What does a bull do?" "What does a bull remind me of?" In this way the dreamer becomes more familiar with the symbol and may discover something that was overlooked.

Dialoguing. Dialoguing with dream symbols provides an opportunity for the dreamer to interact with her inner life and to achieve a working relationship with it. There are a few different approaches to dialoguing. The dreamer may dialogue directly with one of the symbols; or, two or more symbols from the same dream dialogue with each other; or, symbols from different dreams will set up dialogues.

To begin a dialogue with one symbol, the dreamer begins by choosing one dream image to work with. Next, the dreamer either writes an imaginary conversation, or if the dreamer is a young child, it can be done orally. During this process, the dreamer asks the dream symbol questions and then the symbol answers. Some of the questions might be: "Who are you?" "Why are you in my dream?" "What do you have to tell me?" There is no limit as to how many questions can be asked. This process can be very quick or it can be very lengthy.

Creating a Personal Dream Dictionary

Individual images in children's dreams usually serve as the starting point for interpreting their dreams. The context in which individual elements occur and the feelings experienced by the child are both crucial to understanding the meaning. Symbols are personal and universal in nature. Because of this, a child's personal dream dictionary will begin with any symbols, objects, people, locations, and so forth that are already in the child's dreams. If a dream journal has already been started, then it will be easy to see if any dream images repeat themselves. It should be noted that each symbol might have several possible meanings, some negative and some positive. How the child feels *in* the dream and how the child feels *about* the dream will determine the meaning.

There are different ways of going about constructing a dream dictionary. One way is to look at several of the child's dreams. Make a list of all the dream images. Then have the child assign a meaning to each image. For example, if the dream image is a bicycle ask the child what a bicycle means to him. Likely it will be something like fun or freedom. Next to the dream image, write the child's meaning.

According to Garfield (1984), any character (animal or human) that recurs often in children's dreams does so because of the dreamer's emotional involvement - love or hate - with it. The number of times a person dreams about a character may be an index of the strength of the dreamer's feelings about that character (or image). These feelings may be positive or negative ones, depending on the content of the dream.

Another approach to constructing a dream dictionary starts with simply asking the child to define the symbol. For example, if the child dreamed about a horse, you can ask her, "Suppose I were a little kid who had never seen a horse. What would you tell me to help me understand a horse?" The child may want to just show you a picture of a horse, but the conversation shouldn't stop there. Gently coax the child into a description. Projected needs, attitudes, and emotions pour into this reply.

For example, a ten-year-old girl explained that a horse is free. He can run around in his corral, and not be chained up or in the house. Asked to define a cat, one child may emphasize the beauty and graceful movement of the animal; another will stress self-sufficiency; yet another will speak of soft and cuddly qualities. One girl said that cats are sneaky and evil, always licking. The cats appearing in her dreams, therefore, represent a negative presence.

All or none of the responses to a dream symbol may be "correct" by dictionary standards, yet each answer is revealing from a psychological point of view. Often the answers given supply a full understanding of the role that the symbol is assigned.

Chapter 3
What Can Affect Dream Content

Picture thinking is the natural language of our dreaming mind. While awake, we think in words. In sleep we think in images. Whatever is going on in a child's waking life at the moment, will determine dream content. Every experience, every emotion, and every thought will be represented at least partly in the child's nightly dreams (Garfield, 1984). Dreams are visual experiences even though the things we dream about are not being presented to our eyes at the time we are dreaming about them. Occasionally, a stimulus from the external world or from one's own body will be incorporated into a dream.

Pre-sleep Influence

Early childhood fears. Although children have many of the same fears as adults, they also have fears that adults usually don't. Fears of early childhood include fears of falling, of unfamiliar sights and sounds, and an apprehension of losing a parent, just to name a few. The young child is very vulnerable in a world that can suddenly present inexplicable happenings. The child's lack of experience, only tentative ability to distinguish between fact and fantasy, and uncertain apprehension of time sequences tend to make every experience as a passing incident in a life full of incidents. The child is more likely to view an experience as one beyond which there is nothing else (Pitcher & Prelinger, 1963).

Some fears last throughout our lives - fear of the dark, fear of abandonment, fear of attack, fear of punishment or pain, fear of loud noises, fear of drowning and suffocation, fear of animals. As adults, we are generally able to get over our fears, or at least put them aside, hide from them, or learn to live with them. But the fears of small children threaten their very existence, and can render them totally helpless because they are so dependent. It's very important that these childhood fears are not made fun of or turned into a joke (Wiseman, 1989).

41

Watching TV/movies. Another major pre-sleep influence is watching certain types of television programs or movies before going to bed. It is very common to have nightmares after watching scary movies, but can other types of viewing have the same effect, especially for children? Four-year-old Martin started having nightmares after watching a *Power Ranger* video every night before going to bed. One night after waking up crying uncontrollably saying, "I don't want to fight any more!" his parents took away the movie and the nightmares stopped.

Video games. Playing video games has become very popular and may be causing the same effect as watching scary movies. Some of the games that have come on the market recently include vampires, monsters, being chased, killing and being killed. For many of these games the object is to stay alive. Also, frequently these games are interactive instead of the child just being a passive observer as in watching movies. Twelve-year-old Paul dreamed he was a character in a video game being chased by a dragon. Parents should be mindful of the amount of violence in the video games before letting their children play them, especially right before bedtime.

Reading books. Reading books can sometimes have an affect on dreams. Laboratory studies done by David Foulkes (1967) included a 9 year-old boy who had fantastical dreams after reading comic books before going to sleep. The boy's dreams were full of magical birds and kangaroos. Other dreams had negative effects when everyday objects of nature turned into destructive monsters. For example, the boy had dreams about a bug that was transformed into a fearsome giant and then started tearing up the city; a lily when picked by the dreamer turned into a monster and killed a man; and a bird that changed into a monster and ripped up the dreamer's yard.

Another concern about books is making sure they are age appropriate. Books that are meant for adults or older children may be very frightening for young children. Parents should read the book first to make sure the material is suitable. For example, Brenda was in the habit of reading a nighttime story with her children before they went to bed. Her children's ages were Mary 8, Greg 6, and Stacy 4. The children were learning to read and they all took turns. One night they read a story about goblins who kidnapped the main character's baby sister. Although the reading level of the book listed it at 4-8 years, all three children had nightmares for several nights. Even picture books can be very scary to some very young children if they contain pictures of witches, monsters, and teeth baring wild animals.

Worthwhile pre-sleep activities. Parents can provide their children with worthwhile pre-sleep activity. Limit television-viewing time. Instead use that time for activities such as family togetherness, playing games, telling stories, or baking cookies. Avoid television shows that terrorize the child and instead seek out beneficial shows. Even some cartoons are full of violence. Watch the programs with the child and discuss it afterwards to warn off negative effects.

Read books at bedtime. Parents reading out loud can help children develop language skills, their listening comprehension, their imagination, and their social conscience. Research has shown that it also influences their dreams (Garfield, 1984). Bedtime reading selections should be suitable for the level of the child. For very young children just hearing a parent's voice as they read is enough. Toddlers enjoy bright, simple picture books. Older children like books that are associated with their activities and interests.

Provide the child with a protective figure. Sometimes it is helpful for children to imagine a protective shield around their bed as they fall asleep. Children have a need to feel secure at night. Often a boogeyman comes alive from the shadows in the corners of the room. Traditionally this type of protection comes from the concept of a guardian angel, and many children sleep peacefully in the belief that their angel watches over them. Having angel figurines around the bed might make the child feel safe and secure.

Another good idea is to have a good dream reminder before going to sleep. Many parents have a particular prayer they say for the child every night. But parents can also say a good night blessing to help insure good dreams, such as "sweet dreams," "pleasant dreams" or "dream with the angels." Such sayings give a finishing flourish to the going-to-sleep ritual and hopefully sending the child off to dream wonderful dreams.

Emotion. Emotions can have a huge influence on dream content. Robert Van de Castle (1994) contends that dreams act as a mirror to reflect our waking personality. Negative emotions that are felt during the day will resurface at night in dreams. Children can also pick up on emotional disturbances in the home. This can interfere with their sleep and their dreams. It is only natural that if parents are close to their children, they will pick up on the parent's feelings. Empathy can be confusing for a child (Pearce, 1999).

In studies with adults, it has been found that crime in dreams can be the best visual image of high degree of emotion. It's reasonable to expect those same patterns might be true for children's dreams. For example, to kill in a dream may be a sign of extreme hate. To steal can be extreme desire. The enormity of the crime may relate to some trivial event in the dreamer's life, something the dreamer feels guilty about or some action of which they disapprove. A crime dream may also be expressing fear about something the dreamer feels could happen (Chetwynd, 1980).

Depression. Depression can be caused by a variety of reasons and can have a big influence on dream content. In his book *Kids In Danger*, Ross Campbell (1999) explains that children are acutely sensitive to a parent's depression. Depressed behavior by a parent may cause guilt in the child. The child may feel that he is the cause of the parent's depression. Another cause of depression is stress from bereavement. Young children may not understand the concept of death, but they do understand the void that is created in their life from the death of a loved one. The death of a pet can be especially traumatic for a child.

Ten-year-old Harvey dreamed he was in a small room with no windows. He said that in the dream he was bored and depressed. At the time of the dream, he was being disciplined for misbehavior, and his parents had grounded him.

Adult studies done by Cartwright (1992) show that depressive people typically show an unhappy mood and have dreams that are narrow, involve only one dream character (usually the self-character) who repetitiously is failing, deprived, or attacked. Once the depression is lightened, the hostility and anxiety dreams decrease, and there are more harmonious characters in the dreams. Some medications for depression, however, can cause insomnia or nightmares.

Anger. Anger is another strong emotion and pre-sleep influence. Emotions are contagious. When a parent gets angry the child often gets angry also, especially if the parent is angry because the child won't go to bed (Pearce, 1999). A common cause of anger is depression. Young children don't always understand the feelings attached to an emotion and will react to it in anger.

Sometimes anger will show up as a definite dream image. One image that is a common symbol of anger, or fear of one's own anger, is the shark. Sharks usually represent a general sense of threat. The shark's predominant feature is its teeth; the beast threatens to devour and destroy. Dreams portray feelings dramatically and anger can be disguised in the form of a shark or other ferocious wild animal (Garfield, 1984).

Anxiety/Fear. Anxiety dreams are very common in children. Fear is partly instinctual but is largely a learned response. Children often imitate the fears of their parents or their siblings. Fear of the dark is one such learned fear. Children continually go through new developmental stages, each which may cause different types of anxiety. For example, a one-year-old who is learning to walk may be experiencing some separation fears, which may trigger some bad dreams. At this age, there is also a new fear of animals and loud noises.

Sometimes the child has trouble handling the feeling of fear and will dream of the situation symbolically. For example, a mother loses her temper and shouts at her son. The son then dreams of a wicked witch who is threatening him. The boy was reacting to his feeling of fear of harm. He wasn't able to think of his

44

mother in that role, so he used the image of a witch as a substitution for her. His dreaming mind was saying he felt as though his mother was acting like a witch and it was scaring him (Garfield, 1984).

Guilt. Sometimes damaged objects in dreams will symbolize a child's sense of guilt over some waking misbehavior. Guilt in dreams may contain themes of self-reproach and remorse, feelings that can't be expressed in waking life.

Nine-year-old Mary dreamed she was looking at the front of her house. The house had no front wall. Sitting inside was a huge Abraham Lincoln. He took up most of the house. Mary knew that Abraham Lincoln was associated with honesty, and she thought about the "little white lie" she had told her mother the previous day. Maybe it wasn't such a little thing after all.

Sometimes a child is too young to understand the feelings of guilt. Three-year-old Sam woke up crying. He started apologizing to his father saying, "I'm sorry Daddy. I didn't mean to hurt you." Although Sam couldn't remember what the dream was about, it's likely he was feeling guilty about something.

Stress. Stress can come from many areas. Some parents create undue stress in their child's lives without that intention. There is a certain amount of strain built into every parent-child relationship. Anne Wiseman (1989) in *Nightmare Help* writes about how, as a child, her mother would turn her back and leave the room in disappointment at something Anne had done. She stated: "I was totally controlled by that [harmless] gesture. It was perhaps more devastating than being whipped" (p. 22).

Barbara still has memories of when she was young and did something of which her mother disapproved. The mother would tell Barbara that she was "acting ugly" and to go to her room until she could stop being ugly. You can imagine the kinds of emotional turmoil this statement can make on a child, especially if it was repeated every time she was being disciplined. Barbara had frequent nightmares all through childhood.

School is another area that can cause stress in a child. The pressures of constantly being pushed to produce, endless homework, and taking exams can all be extremely stressful. The relationship between the child and teacher and other students can also have an effect on the stress level. It's important to have a harmonious school life. If the child has a large number of bad dreams that take place at school or on the way to school there may be some undue pressure or threat present. Such dreams usually indicate anxiety about school academics, peer problems, or sports activities (Garfield, 1984).

Sibling rivalry can be very stressful at times. There is often a sense of competition for the parents' affection as well as hostility between siblings. Sometimes this conflict shows up in dreams where a sibling is injured, lost or killed. This is common in families that have new babies. The child, once the apple of the parent's eye, now has to share the love and attention with someone else. Dreams of siblings in competition are normal, such as fishing (who gets the bigger fish) or baseball (who hits the ball further) (Foulkes, 1967). If there are feelings of hostility in waking life, there may be dreams of stealing from the sibling or some other crime. A common sibling rivalry dream has the other sibling being punished by the parents, whereby the dreamer gets more of the loving attention for being good.

Grief/Bereavement. Children feel grief at every age. Watch a very young child cry over the loss of a favorite toy or blanket, and you'll see evidence of grieving. Grief may show up in different ways with children, especially with the different ages. Grieving over the loss of a toy is usually short lived. However, loss from a death is a different matter. Again, grieving at different ages will be expressed in different ways. Take for example the death of a pet. An eleven-year-old may express grief through anger, although not directed at anyone in particular. Younger children, such as 4 – 6, may think that death is contagious and will fear their own death or someone else's. Other children, such as ages 7 – 9, may be curious about death and ask questions. Infants on the other hand have no concept of what death is, they usually just think of it as sleeping.

Bereavement can cause dreams about the experience and the accompanying feelings. Many researchers believe that dreaming about painful incidents actually helps the dreamer to cope with what has happened. These dreams help to absorb changes, they strive to make connections with past experiences that may have similar qualities, and they struggle to make sense of questions about the nature of life, death, and the afterlife (Holloway, 2001). Upsetting dreams may be a requisite to an emotional resolution. Repressing these upsetting feelings and dreams may create an impasse in the necessary emotional tumult of working through the grief.

Grief can lead to other emotions, especially fear, which can cause nightmares. Dreams associated with this fear may not be of the actual event, but may contain dream images of animals that are injured or lying dead next to a road. There may also be images of broken toys. A child may feel vulnerable after the death of a very close loved one and have dreams of vacant buildings or empty houses. Another emotion may be of guilt, and the corresponding dreams may include terrifying images of the child's own death (Hartmann, 1998).

Parents can help their children who are coping with the loss of a loved one. John James and Russell Friedman in *When Children Grieve* (2001), say that a death offers the greatest possibility for a parent to teach a child how to deal with loss. Parents should ask themselves how *they* are reacting to the death and then make sure their own behavior is something they want their children to mimic. If the parent is acting strong and hiding sad feelings, the child will do the same. It's a mistake to tell the child not to feel bad, which is dismissing the child's feelings. Parents should instigate a discussion of the death and the feelings involved, starting with their own. Feelings should be acknowledged, not dismissed.

Positive Emotions. Positive emotions are also expressed in children's dreams. Some of these emotions include love, desire, adventures, and sheer animal energy. Some good dream themes may be enjoying a nice activity or a pretty day; playing happily; making an outstanding performance; making new friends; and being loved. There may also be dreams of rhythmic motion - sliding, swinging, dancing, swimming, and flying with pleasure. There may be delicious scents and wonderful music.

Happy dreams can provide solace for a miserable day; they refresh and revive sagging spirits; they offer a chance to practice skills in art and sport; and can create new forms. Good dreams make children feel important, special and loved. They stir a sense of adventure, bring a touch of the magical, and may even give a glimpse of something mystical. Good dreams are fun, and children need them (Garfield, 1984).

Three-year-old Travis woke from a nap laughing. Excitedly he said, "I was playing with Grandma and a frog." Not only was Travis in a happy mood all day, he also got on the phone and called his grandma to tell her about the dream.

Parents can promote good dreams. Try suggesting a good dream before the child goes to sleep. While tucking the child in ask, "What will you dream about tonight?" or "What will be fun?" Then make suggestions, for example, a recent fun vacation or an exciting experience the child recently had. Ask about the dream in the morning so the child knows that you are interested. But never pressure a child to remember a dream.

Another way is to share with the child a funny or joyful dream that you have experienced. Ask if the child has ever had a dream like that. Then suggest that the child have fun by imagining having a similar dream as he falls asleep. Promoting a child's positive dreams will convey a message that good dreams are important. Reinforce them by listening to the child's dreams and then discussing them and by encouraging the child to make a drawing of them. If the child is too young, the parent can make the drawing.

Incorporating the dream content into daily life can be a positive message. Turn the dream into any art form or craft. For example, a dress can be made using a favorite dream image such as a cat. A blanket may have the dream's motif printed on it. If it was an animal dream, wearing a pin of that animal will help the child stay in touch with the magic. Stories and poems can be written based on the dream. Always value a child's good dreams, showing what marvelous adventures can be achieved through dreaming (Garfield, 1984).

Illness

Some dreams can be associated with physical illness. The dreams may vary according to the duration of the illness, its seriousness, and its location, but some common features can be distinguished. At least in adults, we know that illness is associated with an increase in dream recall (Van de Castle, 1994). Illness can cause dreams to become distressful and to include nightmarish or violent images of war, fire, blood, corpses, tombs, raw meat, garbage, dirty water, or references to hospitals, doctors, medicines, and ambulances. These dreams generally appear before the first symptoms of the illness.

A seventeen-year-old girl dreamed that a man with a gun broke through her bedroom window. She was scared to death and tried to escape through the bathroom window. At that point, he shot her on the left side of her head. She woke up with a severe migraine headache on the left side (Warnes & Finkelstein, 1971). This shows the physiological changes that were going on in the girl's head as she slept, which were then incorporated into the dream.

Other dream images associated with headaches include painful sensations in the head; feelings of injury in the head; unpleasant sensations around the eyes; and feelings of pressure on the head. Some themes of headache dreams include being hit on the head with something; hitting the head during an accident; something is obstructing the dreamer's vision; wearing a hat that is too hot; and having lightning strike the dreamer in the head (Garfield, 1991).

Dreams caused by illness are usually longer than distress dreams caused by ordinary annoyances and persist throughout the night and throughout the duration of the illness. The content of the dream can reveal the location and the seriousness of the illness (Van de Castle, 1994). Gastrointestinal disturbances with a slow onset could cause repetitive dreams that involve visions of spoiled food, intestinal worms or rotting and decomposing fish. A pinched muscle may be perceived as a snake that is squeezing the dreamer to death (Hall & Van de Castle, 1966).

A person with a fever may dream of ice cream or ice cubes. A fever can also cause hallucinations and nightmares. Fever dreams can create a variety of dream images, such as excessive body heat or the dream character may be sunburned. There may be raging fires that destroy everything in its path or a fire destroying just one object. These dreams may also be a result of inflammation somewhere in the dreamer's body.

Garfield (1991) says that some dreams can forewarn of an approaching illness. Monitoring your dreams for clues of body disturbances can be of help in identifying diagnostic dreams. Some images to look for are extreme heat, extreme cold, itchiness, and pain. Also pay attention to dreams of any body parts that portray wounding. Additional images to watch for are people, animals, or plants that are injured or dying; buildings or objects that are damaged or destroyed; and machines or equipment that malfunction or break down. Overall, these dreams show damage taking place and impaired functioning. These images don't always symbolize an approaching illness, but they are something to be aware of.

Any child on medication is likely to experience changes in sleep habits and dreams. A great variety of different drugs tend to depress dream time. Sleeping pills (the barbiturates), antidepressants, caffeine, and amphetamines all will suppress dreaming.

There are a few drugs that will increase dreaming time. One such drug is reserpine, used to lower blood pressure. Milk, cheese, and other dairy products all tend to increase the frequency and length of dreaming. Researchers believe that this result is because of a complex interaction between the dream hormone, serotonin, and the high level of tryptophane found in dairy products. This increased dreaming doesn't mean we should give up dairy products. Instead we should enjoy the enhanced dreaming (Garfield, 1984).

Childhood Hospitalization

Being in the hospital can cause a great deal of anxiety for everyone. Hospitalizations can be associated with unhappy dream experiences for a child - both dreams while in the hospital *and* dreams back at home afterwards. To minimize this sort of problem dreaming, some basic principles and methods should be attended to by the parents.

Patients getting ready to undergo surgery have some common dream themes that include loss of mobility, acts of cutting and destruction, and being hurt and injured (Haskell, 1985). Being put under anesthesia can cause hallucinations and nightmares. Some children report dreams of feeling like they are expanding and fear they will blow up. Once a child has had one of these nightmares, it may continue off and on for many years (Garfield, 1984).

For a child who needs to go into the hospital, the parents should give adequate emotional preparation. Being hospitalized is a major life stress for a child. Separated from loved ones and from familiar routines, the child will endure discomfort and pain in an unfamiliar environment; there is a feeling of powerlessness in this setting. By preparing the child for upcoming procedures, parents can prevent some of the inevitable trauma, ensure the child's cooperation, speed recovery, and possibly reduce failure complications.

Garfield suggests using two main approaches to prepare the child for hospitalization: by reading appropriate stories aloud to the child and by making available proper play materials. Both require understanding of the purposes involved and having appropriate discussions with the child. The parent may also need to participate actively in the play. Preparation should begin well before admission, if possible. Throwing children into an unknown situation may trigger fears of being abandoned and fears of being hurt or killed. The purpose of preparation is to assist the child to master fear and pain. By participating in storytelling and play-acting, the child becomes the manipulator instead of the helpless victim.

When looking for appropriate books to read, choose themes that portray the hero or heroine's triumph over danger. The protagonist who is lowly - poor, small, ugly - yet eventually succeeds is particularly inspiring to a hospitalized child who is feeling helpless. Classic examples are the ugly duckling that becomes a swan and David who defeats the giant Goliath. Desirable plots are when the protagonist is passive at first and then learns to solve the problem.

Also good are books that prepare the child for what to expect in the hospital. If possible, select books that relate to the child's specific situation. For example, the book *Madeline*, by Ludwig Bemelmans, tells about the heroine's appendix operation. Share readings that contain characters the child can identify with; stories that tell what to expect, that show bravery in coping with difficulty or inspire the child to live fully. Appendix C contains a list of such books.

The second method involves the use of play. Meaningful preparation requires more than just a verbal explanation; it also requires communication in toys and play - the child's own language. One suggestion for a child that is going to be hospitalized is to make up a game about it. The game may be called "[The child's name] Goes to the Hospital." Using dolls and toys, play out the drama of separation and reunion, supplying lines such as, "Suzy needs to go to the hospital to get well." "Suzy misses Mommy and Daddy." Pretty soon the child will likely join in the game, learning while acting out the upcoming events. This play should also be used when a parent is going to be hospitalized.

Another type of play is to provide material to give expression to the child's feelings in drawings. Paper, pens, crayons, etc. The child can be asked to draw pictures about how it feels to be sick. Parents can make suggestions such as: draw me a picture of yourself now; show me what will happen to you in the hospital; and draw what you will be like afterward. Pictures should not be judged for artistic value. The concern is for the child's feelings. Ask the child to tell a story about the picture. Reflect what the child is feeling. Put it into words. For very young children, or ones who are incapacitated, the parent may need to make the pictures. Ask the child to be the guide, for example, "Here is the little boy that is sick. What happens next? What does the little boy say? What is the little boy feeling?"

For a child unwilling to draw, the parent can suggest putting together a scrapbook or journal of the hospital experience using pictures cut out of magazines. Once the pictures are arranged, ask the child to make up a story. For older children photographs can be taken at different stages of the hospitalization and made into an album that can be shared with friends afterwards.

Toys can also be used as preparation for hospitalization. Depending on the procedure the child will be going through, materials can be provided to show the child what to expect. For example, simple boxes, tubes and wooden tongue depressors can be used to represent intravenous tubing, hose tubes, X-rays, etc. Knowing what to expect can greatly lessen the child's fears.

Other toys can be dolls that represent all of the hospital personnel: nurses, doctors, and technicians, along with patient dolls. Some hospitals have playrooms that are completely set up like a miniature hospital complete with bandages, nurses' caps, doctors' bags, stethoscopes, blood pressure cuffs, thermometers, etc. All of these items help the child play out any anxieties. Parents can clear up any misconceptions the child may have by saying something like: "that's not what's going to happen to you." Parents should always be truthful about the procedures. Sometimes the parents may have to do the playing for the child, letting the child lead the play. Appendix C contains a list of books for parents that give suggestions on preparing children for hospitalization.

External Stimuli

Even though our body is asleep, our minds are still conscious. At this point a strong stimulus will awaken us from sleep. External sensory stimuli that reach us during sleep may become a source of our dreams or be incorporated into them.

Sounds. What kinds of sounds can influence a dreaming child? Parents fighting in another room, a loud television, the telephone ringing, children laughing? Have you ever heard a phone ringing in your dream and then awaken and discover that your phone was actually ringing? A peal of thunder may put us in the midst of a battle. Dreams of war may represent parents warring (Delaney, 1997). The creaking of a door may give us visions of a burglar. A car backfiring outside may appear in the dream as the firing of a gun (Hall & Van de Castle, 1966). Dream of a buzz saw and you may awaken to find someone close by snoring.

Five-year-old Sam, asleep for several hours, suddenly started screaming, "There's a fly in my ear!" Sam's mother examined his ear and found nothing. Then she noticed a buzzing sound and realized there was a rouge mosquito on the loose. It had been buzzing around Sam's ear.

Physical comfort. Unintentional movements during sleep may uncover the

51

body. A boy dreaming of frozen ponds and people ice-skating woke and said his feet and legs were cold (Van de Castle, 1994). If our bedding falls completely off, we may dream we are walking around naked. Lying crosswise on the bed with our feet hanging over the edge may bring a dream of hanging or falling over a cliff. If our head gets under the pillow, there may be a dream of being buried or of being suffocated.

Being in pain may bring dreams of being attacked or injured. Having a sore throat may bring a ghastly dream of being hanged. Falling out of bed could produce a falling dream. It is common to dream that you need to urinate then suddenly awaking and making a mad dash to the bathroom.

A child that is thirsty will likely dream of drinking water or other beverages. Since water is our most basic need, a temporary imbalance in the body may be enough to stimulate drinking dreams. Watery solutions in our bodies dissolve nutrients from foods, distribute them to cells, and carry away waste products. When we drink within our dreams, it is likely our bodies actually require fluid. Dreams of drinking water are often due to a real thirst. If a child experiences frequent dreams of drinking water, it may be due to a large intake of salt in the diet (Garfield, 1984).

Likewise, if a child goes to bed hungry there may be dreams of eating. Luscious cakes, mounds of cookies, and heaps of candy are favorite treats for children. There may be dreams of cooking, grocery shopping or picking food from a garden. Many of these dreams have other people doing the action. For example, "Mommy was grocery shopping" or "Mommy was picking vegetables." The particular type of food being eaten may be an indication of something the body needs. For example, if an orange is being consumed it may be a physical need for vitamin C; eating red meat may be a sign of a need for more protein in the diet; and eating broccoli may be a sign for more calcium.

Riding in a vehicle. While taking a road trip, four-year-old Nelson awoke from a nap saying he dreamed he was in a racecar, sitting on his father's lap, going around the track. Since his father is a racecar driver, Nelson knew what riding around the track felt like. The motion of the car in which he was riding produced a similar feeling and then created the dream.

Being touched. Four-year-old Simmy awoke with a start: "I dreamt that a monster grabbed me by the foot!" Simmy's father had been gently tugging on his foot to wake him up for preschool. We've probably all experienced this. Being awakened from a sound sleep by someone touching us, often creates a feeling of fear and confusion.

Odors. A strong smelling substance may stimulate the mucous membrane of the

52

dreamer's nose. Perfume scents in the room may bring dreams of flowers. Likewise, the scent of flowers may bring images of certain people associated with that scent.

Water. While conducting laboratory studies, David Foulkes (1982) would sprinkle water on the face or scalp of the sleeping child. Immediately awakening the child, a dream would be reported that would often have some association to wetness. Some examples included fish swimming in a bowl, a flowing river, and that it was raining.

Birth Order

In a study done by Robert Van de Castle (1994) about young adults, he found that first-born females dreamed of more aggressive characters and more aggressive interactions with strangers than did younger siblings. Middle-born females (with at least one older and one younger sibling) had more friendly characters and more strangers performing friendly acts towards the dreamer. Unlike the males in the study, females generally report more children and babies in their dreams, but-last born females, the "babies" of their own families, had fewer children and babies in their dreams than females in other birth order positions.

When birth order for male dreamers was studied, it was found that first-born male college students had more themes of "positive interaction" than did younger siblings. First-born males may have more dreams where they are in leadership roles, more adventurous, or being a father image. Younger siblings may have dreams of following a leader, following the rules, or being a part of a group.

Sex Of The Child

Sex differences can be apparent in dreams from earliest childhood. Young boys dream about games such as fighting and playing war while young girls dance and play with dolls. These differences become more pronounced with age and are demonstrated, for example, by the emphasis females give to items such as clothing and to feelings. It seems the child's wish is to become a competent adult. Sometimes these wishes are acted out in dreams, and other times they are acted out in everyday behavior (Foulkes, 1967).

We know that the symbolism of play resembles the symbolism of the dream (Piaget & Inhelder, 2000). These sex differences can also be seen in the waking state as reported in the book *Children Tell Stories*. Pitcher and Prelinger (1963) tell us that at the ages of two to five years boys talk more about objects of transportation, insects, and objects of nature than girls do. They also include more occupational figures, more individual objects, and somewhat more characters in general.

Girls, on the other hand, tend to present people more vividly and realistically, and to identify themselves with the personalities and experiences of others. Girls often quote conversations they have heard. Whereas boys seldom name their characters, girls always have a ready supply of names for everything.

The location in dreams is as important as the stage set of a play. Settings reflect the interests, tastes, and resources of the people who inhabit them. Familiar places, especially the dreamer's home and the homes of friends and other family members, occur more often in the dreams of socially passive and dependent boys as well as in the majority of girl's dreams. Dream props will also be different in most children's dreams (Garfield, 1984).

The dream settings for most girl's dreams are set in their own homes, most frequently in the kitchen, the bedroom, and the living room. Girls are usually homebodies in their dreams, having tea parties and playing with their dolls. Girl's dreams also contain frequent references to household objects: beds, pillows, clothes, fabric, books, etc. Vehicles in girls' dreams are usually very simple: a boat, a car, a truck. Girls dream more often of clothing than boys do. They are also more social, often describing the face, hair and eyes of their dream characters.

Boy's dreams usually take place outdoors, in the mountains, in the woods, or in a field. The dreams are usually full of implements. Guns, swords, bows and arrows, bombs, and other deadly weapons may be seen frequently. Vehicles are seen more often in boy's dreams than in the girl's and are usually greatly varied: airplanes, helicopters, racecars, speedboats, rockets, and spaceships. When describing things, boys usually refer to the size, speed, and intensity.

<u>Menstrual cycle.</u> Although most of the studies about dreaming and menstrual cycles involve adult women, some of the findings are probably relevant to teenage girls also. Dreams during the menstrual cycle frequently include blood and babies. The color red is also common: red chairs, red beds, red towels, etc. How the female feels about the menstrual cycle could also determine the dream themes. A young girl may have a different reaction than an adult woman, such as fear and confusion (Van de Castle, 1994).

Birth of a baby is a common theme during the menstrual cycle, but death is also fairly common. It could be because of an unconscious awareness that the blood represents the absence of a potential baby. Birth and death, representing the beginning and end of life, appear to be closely linked during menstruation. Another pair of opposites is femininity and masculinity. Menstruation is undeniably one activity that differentiates the two sexes. Menstruation can be considered the hallmark of femininity and a time when female's special biological functioning is emphasized. This is also the time when themes of marriage, weddings, and engagements become prominent in dreams.

In the studies done by Van de Castle it was found that when a woman is ovulating, her dreams tend to be friendlier toward males than towards females. But when she starts to menstruate, her dreams will show greater friendliness towards females.

Females who experience premenstrual water retention may have dreams of large bodies of water such as oceans. There may also be dreams of swimming. Huge balloons may represent swelling or the dreamer may see herself as putting on weight or becoming fat, wearing clothes that are too tight, or sitting in a small enclosed place.

The dream sometimes allows us to look into the depths and folds of our very being — mainly a closed book in states of consciousness. It gives us such valuable insight into ourselves, such instructive revelations of our half-hidden emotional tendencies and powers that, were we awake, we should have good reason to stand in awe of the demon who is apparently peering at our cards with the eyes of a falcon.

— F.W. Hildebrant - German psychologist in the 1800s

Chapter 4
Dreams Change With Age

Dreams may represent the development of the child's ego, not by age, but by continuous developmental process. As stated before, the content of a dream is determined by the person's personality and by the events and experiences of the waking life. Children's dreams mirror the state of their developing personality. If they are developing emotionally, socially and cognitively without any problems, then their dreams will be full of happy and creative events and feelings. If their dreams contain disturbing images or emotions, then it may be that they are encountering some sort of problem in their personal development. Careful exploration of the dream can help determine which aspect is causing the problem (Spurr, 1999).

Imaginal Skills

Children's imaginal skills increase with age. With increasing experience and knowledge, there is a growing sense of personal mastery. There is an expansion in the spatial dimension stretching from the body to the immediate surroundings. They are acquiring larger maps of the world, or "cognitive maps." For example, the two-year-old places happenings within the home property, while by the age of five the average boundaries of space have stretched beyond familiar places; toward foreign countries, the sea, the sky and towards less definite, half-imaginary places such as just "forests" and "mountains." There is a slight but consistent tendency for boys to show more expansion in space then girls do (Pitcher & Prelinger, 1963).

As the child ages there is an increasing awareness of people (including the self) as having consistent identities. However, as the child ages, the main character in dreams may become less clearly identifiable. This may be because the child's waking world is filled more with groups of people, many of them strangers. For example, a two-year-old will usually only focus on one person, such as the mother or father. An older child, however, will be going to school and attending other so-

57

cial events, therefore interacting with more people.

The inner complexity of the dream characters will change with age. This may reflect the child's awareness of inner complexity within the self as well as in others, which could indicate a process of differentiation within the ego. An inner differentiation at this point would mean that a person or a character (such as an animal or object) does not simply act as a whole, but rather shows an interplay with at least one other component (Pitcher & Prelinger, 1963).

The range of activity or passivity of the dream characters increases with the child's age. As children are able to master their own actions and more immediate environment, their dream characters are also able to master the same things. The dreams start to show more activity rather than passivity (In this case "passivity" refers to what happens to the dream character). This is seen mostly in boys, and it increases with age. With girls, however, passivity increases with age.

Children show an increase in imaginative qualities as they age. They are better at telling stories and their dreams reflect this. As the child becomes better related to reality, there will be less need for reassurance and the imagination can flow freely. Increased use of imagination shows that the child is learning to control ego drives, a development that comes as the ego defenses are firmly established. Increased imagination shows a greater inner differentiation and a greater internalization process. Increasing use of imagination shows a more mature expression of the ego, which reflects a functioning in response to varying stimuli from within as well as from the outside.

According to Pitcher & Prelinger (1963) the two-year-old's range of characters is generally confined to the immediate home environment. The characters are usually fluid, in the sense that a dream character starts out to be an animal but ends up being the child. At the age of two the child's dream characters are familiar from waking life – home, parents, other family members and pets. Objects in the dream also reflect experience in waking life, such as cars and trains, etc.

The three-year-old's dream characters will have a greater variety than the two-year-old's will. There will be the inclusion of fanciful characters commonly associated with fairy tales such as witches, giants, ghosts and princesses. There is a belief in magic. The people involved spread further from the home, such as police and firemen. Animals in dreams become wilder such as squirrels, snakes, frogs and sharks. They understand the past and the future. They acknowledge the difference between fact and fiction.

Four and five-year-olds will increase the dream characters even more. As their world expands, so do their dreams. They are more aware of the different seasons, and time will now have meaning. They are also learning that there is a world out in space and will have knowledge of the sun, moon and stars. Magic intensifies in their dreams. There will be more interactions between the dream characters as they understand what relationships are. They know what cause and effect means and what is real and unreal.

Ego Development

A decisive issue in the development and secure establishment of a functioning ego is the definition of its relation to reality. In a sense, it could be said that at first everything is "real" to the child, that later a child learns to discriminate between the real and unreal - or, better, between what is real externally and what is real only in her thoughts (Pitcher & Prelinger, 1963). A third phase of the development of one's relation to reality is reached when unreality, also recognized as such, is put to resourceful use. The content of children's dreams, like their play, may be rehearsal for the next developmental roles.

Cognitive stages in children. The cognitive stages are the development of the thought processes. Swiss theoretician Jean Piaget built theories about cognitive development. Piaget believed that changes in children's thought processes result in a growing ability to acquire and use knowledge about their world. Piaget described cognitive development as occurring in a series of stages. At each stage a new way of thinking about and responding to the world develops. Each stage constitutes a qualitative change from one type of thought or behavior to another, building on the stage before it and constructing the foundation for the one that comes next. All people go through the same stages (which have many facets) in the same order, even though the timing varies from one person to another, making any age cutoff only approximate.

Piaget believed that the core of intelligent behavior is a person's inborn ability to adapt to the environment. Children build on their sensory, motor, and reflex capacities to learn about and act upon their world. As they learn from their experiences, they develop more complex cognitive structures. At each stage of development, a person has his or her individual representation of the world (Papalia, 1996).

A child's dream thinking will not be more cognitively complex than their waking thinking. The development of a child's competence as a dream-maker closely parallels his developing competence as a waking thinker (Foulkes, 1978). A child's dreams then will correspond to the developmental stage that he is going through.

Sensorimotor Stage. (Birth to 2 years) The infant changes from a being that responds primarily through reflexes to one who can organize activities in relation to the environment. The child learns through sensory and motor activity. In this stage children become aware that they exist apart from objects and other people. There is also a recognition that certain events cause other events.

Dreams at this stage will consist mainly of feeling states. For example, the dreams may be of hunger, thirst, physical and emotional comfort, and a general peacefulness. Unpleasant dreams may be the result of those needs not being met. Very young children never include themselves in dreams, says Sylvia Browne (2002). The reason this is so is because they don't yet have a sense of their own identities.

Preoperational Stage. (2 to 7 years) The child develops a representational system and uses symbols such as words to represent people, places, and events. In this stage, children can think about something without needing to see it in front of them. Children can understand and count numbers and are able to classify objects, people and events into meaningful categories. They understand cause and effect and have empathy for other people's feelings. In this stage it also becomes possible to explain and predict other people's actions by imagining their beliefs, feelings, and thoughts. In the preoperational stage, dreams are episodic and distractible rather than sustained. What organization they have derives from a momentarily appearing body stimulus or a discrete memory from the previous day.

According to Foulkes (1978), at ages three and four, dream reports are quite brief, just a sentence or two, and are usually lacking in dynamic, interactive qualities, and feelings. At this age there is not much organization nor inner coherence, but in general they are not very imaginative. There is usually motivational themes that tend to be related to body functions (such as thirst and hunger), rather than to interpersonal interactions.

By the ages of five and six, children's dream reports have more than doubled in length and have become markedly more dynamic and interactive in their content. Dreams will now have a definite, usually simple, story line. The child becomes more active in the dreams during this age. The dreams themselves seem to be in transition from the preoperational stage to operational. They no longer have a flat, static quality of the three- and four-year old's dreams, but are more like vignettes, or imaginary "slices of life." However, they are not yet fully elaborate fantasies (Foulkes, 1978).

Concrete Operations. (7 to 12 years) Children can solve problems logically if they are focused on the here and now. During this stage, children are less egocentric, and they are able to apply logical principles to actual (concrete) situations. They can use internal mental operations (thinking) to solve problems. Children are better at dealing with numbers, understanding the concepts of time and space, distinguishing reality from fantasy, and classifying objects.

Seven- and eight-year-olds generally have achieved an internally integrated, "operational" organization of their waking thoughts, and their dreams also have improved in formal operations. Subplots are balanced against one another and scenarios as a whole begin to reflect clear narrative intentions. Enduring childhood concerns begin to organize dream content in relatively complex and personally meaningful ways. The most prevalent of these themes is usually the child's wish to become a competent adult. Sometimes these themes are enacted in relatively realistic imagery of everyday play behavior or the child begins to invent novel situations using imaginative story lines.

At the ages of 9 through 11, children's dreams have started to focus on themselves. The child is able to see himself and his own actions more clearly without the defensive actions that are used during waking time. The child is able to confront emotional issues. There will also be a stronger connection with the same sex parent. Boys will have dreams of interaction with the father figure as the mother figure begins to fade into the background. Likewise, the girls begin a stronger identification with the mother as the father image begins to fade into the background (Foulkes, 1967).

By late preadolescence (ages 11 and 12), children's formal powers of dream organization have become well consolidated, and the content of their dreams has become as purposeful, realistic, and as benign as it probably ever will be. Although each dream seems to contain at least one kernel that is bizarre or contextually inexplicable, there is generally a sex specific plausibility for each overall scenario. For example, girls are focusing on female dream characters and on sex-typed feminine activities (Foulkes, 1978).

Formal Operations. (12 years through Adulthood) This is the highest level of cognitive development. The person can think in abstract terms, deal with hypothetical situations, and think about possibilities. Attaining formal operations gives adolescents a new way to manipulate - or operate on - information. In the earlier stage of concrete operations, children could think logically only about the concrete, the here and now. In this stage, adolescents are no longer so limited. They can now deal with abstractions, test hypotheses, and see infinite possibilities.

In early adolescence (ages 13 to 14), there are signs that dream imagery is becoming thematically more obscure and formally more complex. Family characters and settings are less prominent than before. There is less literal usage of familiar people and places in constructing dream scenarios, and the scenarios contain fewer instances of concretely enacted "physical" activity. While manual and locomotor activity are still most important in sustaining dream themes, the role of speech is growing at this age. For example, there is more verbal interaction between characters.

At this age certain classes of "positive" and "negative" feelings, motives, and

61

outcomes show shifts consistent with the adolescent developmental stage. For example, at this age the number of dreams in which characters approach one another socially decreases significantly. However, dreams are still full of fantasy imagery. Social approach themes occur more often than social-attack themes, and dreamers are more likely to receive friendly than hostile acts initiated by others.

<u>Children's dreams show that dream making is a mental skill that is subject to the same developmental patterning as any waking mental skill.</u> "Crazy," dreamlike thinking is something young children are not able to execute very well, but they get successively better at it as they pass through the stages of cognitive development. Cognitive development places many constraints on the nature of such symbolism. Children's dreams indicate that their ability to conceptualize external reality and their own feelings undergoes definite developmental elaboration (Foulkes, 1978).

<u>Psychosocial stages in children.</u> Psychosocial stages of development include the development of drives and of motives derived from them. Also included is the development of physical apparatuses for their discharge, their channeling, and their control, and the gradual accumulation of experience in relation to the gratification of these needs and drives. Among them particularly will be interpersonal relationships and generalized thinking that later evolves into individualized thinking.

The general trend leads away from processes centering on the body and its needs toward phenomena that are increasingly socially oriented around the relationships with other people and with the surrounding culture (Pitcher & Prelinger, 1963). As age progresses, children use a more detailed process of thinking and of feeling to the characters in their dreams. This will most generally be seen as children reach the age of 5. <u>The dream may be seen as a basic attempt to master contemporary problems of social adjustment.</u>

Erik Erikson, a German-born psychoanalyst, believed that the major theme throughout life is the quest for identity, which he defined as a basic confidence in one's inner continuity amid change. In his developmental formulations, Erikson describes the prominent themes, which become apparent in the behavior of growing individuals at different stages and emphasizes their over-determination (extreme persistence). These themes evolve from an interplay of drives, of developing skills and abilities, and of environmentally derived experience. The fact that the people living around a growing child respond to his biologically maturing needs in specific ways, and the fact that the child's developing capacities interact with his experience and with his needs in certain ways, lead to the manifestation of specific "issues" at different stages of development.

Trust vs. Mistrust. (Birth to 12 months) This issue centers in the drive theme of orality (eating, drinking, etc.) and around the related interpersonal phenomena of mothering, of support, comfort, and protection, and around the basic emotional orientation and outlook on the world that develops out of experiences with the various aspects of gratification of bodily needs. Essential interpersonal expectations are formed around experiences of satisfaction or deprivation, particularly in their recurrent aspects. Thus evidence of trust or of mistrust can be found in a variety of areas which may differ from person to person (Erikson, 1958).

In the second part of the first year, the child goes through three developments: (1) a physiological one where the child experiences a general tension associated with a more violent drive to incorporate, appropriate, and observe more actively (along with the discomfort of "teething"); (2) a psychological one where the infant becomes increasingly aware of the self as a distinct person; and (3) an environmental one with the mother's apparent turning away from the baby toward pursuits which she had given up in late pregnancy and postnatal care. The ratio and relation of basic trust to basic mistrust established during early infancy determines much of the individual's capacity for simple faith (Erikson, 1959).

This is also the age when a lot of infants begin going to a daycare facility. Six-month-old Tracey began having nightly screaming episodes after beginning fulltime daycare. He would scream and twist and kick until his parent's brought him into their bed. He would sleep fitfully for an hour or so and then begin screaming again. At this point nothing could console him and eventually the entire family would fall asleep out of total exhaustion. Although Tracey seemed to enjoy being in daycare, it's possible he was feeling a sense of abandonment from his mother who had previously spent every moment with him. These feelings may have been a cause of nightmares for Tracey. At this age his dreams would be more of feelings than images. His nightly screaming fits continued for about a year.

Autonomy vs. Shame and Doubt. (12-18 months to 3 years) This issue, in the drive area, centers in anality and its modes of elimination and retention. Psychosocially it involves problems of social regulation of bodily needs and consequently problems of conformity or of negativism and resistance. The "negative phases" of various developmental theories belong to the time period in which this issue is prominent. In this stage is the development of what will later become the person's will, in its variations of willpower and willfulness (Erikson, 1958).

In this stage, the child undergoes "toilet training" whereby there will be a sense of independence or the showing of defiance and stubbornness. The resolution of this issue will determine whether the individual is apt to be dominated by a sense of autonomy, or by a sense of shame and doubt. Dreams during this stage may reflect these feelings.

Children under the age of two often wet the bed as well as a majority of three-year-olds. If the child is having trouble with bed wetting there may be anxiety themes or nightmares. Imagery may contain characters laughing at the dreamer. There may be feelings of shame or guilt by the dreamer or other dream characters. There may be a sense of being watched or of feeling alone in a difficult situation (Spurr, 1999).

Three-year-old Maurice dreamed he was sitting in the middle of his bed, which was standing in his front yard. Several of his friends surrounded him. They were laughing and pointing at him. He looked down and saw that he had wet the bed.

Initiative vs. Guilt. (3 to 6 years) This issue, corresponding to the phallic stage of libidinal development, is, on the side of the ego, also determined by increasing mastery and use of the locomotor apparatuses. Children at this stage explore, get into things, intrude, experiment, and try to master simple challenges. The emphasis, especially in boys, is, according to Erikson, on "making" in the sense of appropriation and even usurpation. The assertion of the self, which in the preceding phase occurred primarily in terms of a static delimitation of an autonomous domain of being and acting, takes place now in an expanding and, so-to-speak, imperialistic form.

A successful experience in this stage will result in traits of enterprise, of activity, and of confidence in relation to the world which becomes perceived as something manageable and as something that can be successfully exploited. If in the growing child's experience with others, he is made to feel that he is not to disturb things, that the aggressive aspects of exploration and intrusion are condemnable, and that he is dangerous or at least a bother, then guilt may be the outcome of this phase. The phallic orientation of the libido during this period heightens the subjective importance of intrusive body parts and functions so that prohibitions of intrusive behavior tend to be subjectively perceived by the child as threats of body damage and ultimately castration. For this reason there are, in the definition of the Initiative vs. Guilt scale, criteria referring to body damage as indicators of guilt.

Children at this age are usually beginning primary school, which is a critical transition point in childhood. Enduring personality characteristics have already been established and these, in part, will determine how the child negotiates the new demands of being in school. Their dreams will be a good indicator of their initial reaction to school and where they may need help in adjusting. Dreams that show good adaptation will have themes that are positive and without anxiety. There may be themes of challenges, such as climbing large steps or trees and scaling walls or fences (Spurr, 1999).

Other dreams at this age may show a sense of curiosity. Non-threatening, complicated buildings such as palaces and grand buildings usually represent natural curiosity. There may be dreams of following a path through the woods or running through a flower garden. Dreams may show a specific interest the child may have developed such as rock collecting. If the child is reading a book in the dream, it is a good indication the child is ready to begin reading in waking life.

Six-year-old Helen dreamed that a whale swallowed her and her friend, Bess. They were very scared and somehow Helen's arm got cut. By working together, Helen and Bess were able to get themselves out of the whale.

Industry vs. Inferiority. (6 years to Puberty) This issue is the ego - psychological counterpart to the latency period in libidinal development. In this stage, the child becomes able and eager to learn systematically and to collaborate with others (Erikson, 1958). The relatively decreased intensity of libidinal demands during this phase and the correspondingly diminished importance of particular, libidinally charged objects, allow the child to turn more toward the world of things. The child's access to them has been assured during the preceding period of intrusiveness. Now the child organizes his exploits and becomes familiar with them.

School readiness arises from the freedom to attend to things, both material and abstract, which arises at a time when also adaptive capacities of a psychomotor and intellectual sort have reached a certain stage of maturation. The accomplishments of society in the form of technological skills, of production, knowledge, and learning, confront the growing child at this stage and are beginning to be mastered. Playing becomes more concerned with "things" than merely with the practice and exercise of body functions.

Dreams at this stage will show how the child adapts to situations in waking life. Children will be dealing with increased schoolwork, which may be difficult to master. There may be dream themes of impossible obstacles or dangerous conditions. At this stage there is also an increase in social activity, consisting of making and interacting with friends. If the child is having trouble with certain peers, there may be dreams containing threatening dream characters or themes of running and hiding.

At this stage children are also learning how to control their own emotions. Some children find it difficult to monitor their aggressive impulses. One moment they are playing happily and the next moment they are lashing out at someone who has upset them. Left unchecked, aggressive behavior can cause them to be shunned by their peers, resulting in feelings of rejection and then more anger. The child may become depressed because of his feeling like he's out of control. Dreams can symbolize these feelings with imagery of something out of control (such as a car) or aggressive wild animals. There may be feelings of being trapped with no escape (Spurr, 1999).

Seven-year-old Marco often displayed aggressive behavior in waking life and didn't seem to have any friends. He had a nightmare where he was thrashing around, out of control. He felt as if he were trapped like a wild animal. There were shadowy shapes around him, but they would not communicate. This made Marco angry. Marco kicked out and the shadowy shapes disappeared, leaving Marco all alone and feeling isolated. The dream shows that Marco's aggression had caused his isolation (Spurr, 1999).

Identity vs. Identity Confusion. (Puberty to Young Adulthood) This issue centers around an adolescent's own sense of identity. The chief task of adolescence is to resolve the conflict of identity versus identity confusion - to become a unique adult with a meaningful role in life. To form an identity, the ego organizes a person's abilities, needs, and desires and helps to adapt them to the demands of society.

In adolescence, the search for "who I am" becomes especially insistent, as the young person's sense of identity begins where the process of identification ends. In this stage, the adolescent must determine his own sense of self (identity), including the role he will play in society. One of the most crucial aspects in the search for identity is deciding on a career (Papalia, 1996).

Dreams during this stage may involve issues of self-esteem. If a child is having trouble with this issue there may be dreams of hiding or of trying to hide the face. There may be themes of being singled out in front of a group of people, of being made fun of or some other embarrassing situation. Dreams such as these can undermine the child's self-confidence in waking life (Spurr, 1999).

Ten-year-old Tiffany dreamed that her teacher yelled at her to come to the front of the class. Tiffany's fear caused her to put her hands up in front of her face, trying to hide. The teacher yelled, "It's game time!" He grabbed her and started spinning her around. Everyone in the class stared at her causing Tiffany extreme embarrassment.

Chapter 5
Nightmares

Nightmares are long, frightening dreams that will usually wake the sleeper. The nightmare is normally a very complicated dream that gets more terrifying towards the end. Upon awakening, the person may be breathing rapidly and there will be an increase in heart rate. Sometimes upon awakening the dreamer is literally frozen with fear. Nightmares are often called anxiety dreams and are very common in children, although they rarely require treatment. Talking or striking out during the dream rarely occur. However, the dreamer may dream that he is screaming, but usually the screaming is not out loud. Usually the content of a nightmare will be vividly recalled.

The dreamer may feel any number of disturbing emotions in a nightmare, such as anger, guilt, sadness or depression, but the most common feelings are fear and anxiety. Almost always in a nightmare, the sleeper is in some way vulnerable, such as being chased, hurt, attacked, or killed. Sleepwalking or thrashing about is usually not a part of nightmares. For many people, the term nightmare is used in a generic way to describe a "bad" dream or a dream associated with overwhelming anxiety and apprehension. They are a safe way to experience bad things.

It is important to distinguish between being frightened *by* a dream and being frightened *in* the dream. Being frightened *by* a dream is more common with early childhood. In laboratory studies (Foulkes, 1982), it seemed that many of young children's frightening dreams represented not anxiety experienced *in* sleep but anxiety experienced during slow and imperfect arousal *from* sleep. The potentially frightening dream imagery and/or the external darkness and internal confusion in which it is recalled evoke an emotional response. One example is being wakened suddenly or abruptly. There is often a state of confusion where the sleeper is half-awake and half-asleep. It could take several minutes to wake the child completely.

Nightmares usually occur in the second two-thirds of the night, normally just before waking. They happen most commonly as part of a developmental phase between the age of 2 and the teenage years. The nightmares of early childhood likely reflect the struggle to learn to deal with normal childhood fears and problems. Nightmares generally decrease with age, and are usually a passing phase.

Studies done (Leach, 2000) show that nearly half of all toddlers wake up during the night afraid. The waking is due to some type of nightmare, but at that age the child is not able to describe the dream. Some children wake up terrified several times each night for a while and then not at all for months. The waking may take the form of instant panic, so that the child is sitting bolt upright in the crib, clearly terrified. On other occasions the child is crying as if something dreadful had happened. Studies have shown that the sleep disturbances of infants in the first year of life may be wordless nightmares (Siegel & Bulkeley, 1998).

Nightmares introduce us to some strong feelings. They may tell us that we are feeling scared, alone, helpless, weak, frightened or left out. Sometimes these are new feelings - feelings so big they make us tremble, scream, fall out of bed, or cry for help. Nightmares are designed to wake us up. Nightmares make us sit up and listen (Wiseman, 1989).

Nightmares occur more often if a child is anxious or stressed. A traumatic event, a frightening television program or movie or some medicines can lead to nightmares. Many nightmares may seem to have no obvious cause and no special significance. However, if the same nightmare recurs night after night, there will be a meaning for the child (Pearce, 1999). Trying to understand the nightmare will help a parent understand the child's fears and anxieties.

Most nightmares are a normal part of coping with changes in life. They are not necessarily a sign of pathology and may even be a positive indication that the person is actively coping with a new challenge. For children, this could occur in response to such events as entering school, moving to a new neighborhood or living through a parent's divorce or remarriage. Nightmares in children are reactions to upsetting events, situations and relationships. Nightmares will diminish in intensity and frequency as the child and family recover and cope with the stress (Siegel & Bulkeley, 1998).

Often the dream appears as a metaphor, which disguises our own identity or the focus of our anger, fears, or desires. When the dream comes in a voice so strong that it cannot be ignored, we call it a nightmare. Like a shout for help, it demands attention. The dream messenger is saying that something is out of balance, or it forces a look at feelings that are not acknowledged in waking life. Sometimes nightmares feel like it is a question of life and death. Time is needed to process the feelings that this kind of dream brings, otherwise, the dream will just grow louder and nastier, and keep recurring. (Wiseman, 1989).

Night Terms

During night terrors, children awaken in a delirium accompanied by great fear. The frequency decreases as the child grows older. The night terror usually occurs during the deepest part of sleep, usually within the first couple of hours. The dreamer becomes agitated and appears to be awake but isn't. The dreamer seems very frightened, with rapid breathing and a fast heart rate. It can be very scary for the parent and cause a great deal of anxiety, probably more so than for the child because there is usually no memory of it in the morning (Owen & Millman, 2000).

With a nightmare or anxiety-producing dream the dreamer usually has a very detailed recall of the content. A night terror, on the other hand, usually will produce little or no dream recall. If there is any recall it is generally just a fragment or a single frightening image. Often it is the feeling that something or someone is sitting on the dreamer's chest, or that someone scary is in the room (Hartmann, 1987). A scream may precede the awakening and there could be a long period of disorientation after awakening, which may include uncontrollable crying. It is often difficult to completely awaken a child from a night terror.

During a night terror great autonomic nervous system changes take place very rapidly. The pulse and respiratory rates sometimes double and the blood pressure may rise. Because the awakening is so abrupt and involves such extraordinary shifts in the autonomic nervous system, night terrors have been classified as "disorders of arousal." Sleepwalking sometimes follows the onset of night terrors (Van de Castle, 1994). There may also be thrashing about which could cause injury to the dreamer and others.

According to Foulkes (1978), the explanation of night terrors may lie in physiology. There may be a kind of unconscious "panic" response to the slowing of life functions - heart rate, blood pressure, respiration - that occurs during sleep.

Possible Causes Of Nightmares And Night Terrors

Excessive tiredness/sleep deprivation. Night terrors, especially, are usually aggravated by excessive tiredness or sleep deprivation. Sleep deprivation can cause the person to become agitated and experience changing emotions. Although some parents believe that tiring a child during the day will help the child sleep better, an overtired child is more likely to have a bad dream (Leach, 2000).

Stress. Nightmares tend to be more frequent and more frightening at times of change and times of stress. Situations that make the sleeper feel helpless or vulnerable may be triggers for nightmares (Hartmann, 1987).

In *Understanding Your Child's Dreams*, Pam Spurr (1999) gives some examples of nightmares caused by stress:

- Bereavement over the death of a pet. Children under four often appear quite unaffected about bereavement. Usually they are more unsettled by the sight of others grieving than by the thought that they will never see a treasured pet or relative again. Children over four have a more developed understanding of time and what it might mean that someone is "never coming back"; they feel bereavement deeply. Losing a pet is frequently a child's first experience of death.
- Stress caused by schoolwork. At school the pressure to provide more detailed work increases with age. Some children find the challenge daunting.
- Being bullied by other kids. Being subjected to bullying terrifies many children. They are often afraid to tell their parents or teachers in fear that it will get back to the bullies and the experience will increase. They may also be afraid that the bully will carry out a threat, and that they will be injured.
- Stress caused by bedwetting. Children going through the process of toilet training are often frustrated by their lack of control. The parent needs a lot of patience during this time. Children vary considerably in the speed with which they learn to use the toilet. External factors (such as teasing) from others can also affect the process.

Another example that could cause nightmares is experiencing stress after being a witness to parents having sex. Pitcher & Prelinger (1963) report a nightmare by four-year-old Noreen who described the dream: "A man throwed a piano at my mommy...And then he threw a little piece of choo-choo train into my mouth, and my legs were shivering. And I pretended like I was dying, but I wasn't...and then he made me do some tricks...I could really feel my legs shivering..." (p. 236). It's interesting that the dream starts out with the girl's mother going through the experience and then it turns into herself.

Anxiety. No one is totally insulated from anxiety-producing events or situations. Most children are vulnerable to fears and uncertainties as a part of growing up, and most children encounter many normal developmental steps and environmental demands that challenge their adaptation skills. Any radical change in a toddler's life may cause anxiety whether he shows it during the day or not. There are some types of anxiety that are beyond the ordinary and are classified as disorders.

The first disorder is Separation Anxiety Disorder. It describes children who have unrealistic fears, are oversensitive, self-conscious, have nightmares and experience chronic anxiety. These children lack self-confidence, are apprehensive in new situations, and tend to be immature for their age. Children with this disorder are often described by their parents as shy, sensitive, nervous, submissive, easily discouraged, worried, and frequently moved to tears. Typically, they are overly dependent, particularly on their parents. The essential feature of this disorder involves excessive anxiety about separation from major attachment figures, such as mother, and from familiar home surroundings. In most cases, a clear psychosocial stressor can be identified, such as the death of a pet or relative (Carson, 1992).

When children with separation anxiety disorder are actually separated from their significant others, they typically become preoccupied with morbid fears, such as the worry that their parents are going to become ill or die. They cling helplessly to attachment figures, have difficulty sleeping, and become intensely demanding. Separation anxiety can relate back to Erikson's psychosocial stage of trust vs. mistrust.

The second disorder is Generalized Anxiety Disorder. It is characterized by chronic excessive worry, traditionally described as free-floating anxiety. This disorder is common and can cause nightmares. Children who have anxiety disorders may exhibit some of the following factors:
1. An unusual constitutional sensitivity, an easy ability to be conditioned by aversive stimuli, and a buildup and generalization of "surplus fear reactions."
2. The undermining of feelings of adequacy and security by early illnesses, accidents, or losses that involved pain and discomfort. The traumatic effect of such experiences is often due partly to such children finding themselves in unfamiliar situations, as during hospitalization. The traumatic nature of certain life changes, such as moving away from friends and into a new situation, can have an intensely negative effect on a child's adjustment.
3. The "modeling" effect of an overanxious and protective parent who sensitizes a child to the dangers and threats of the outside world. Often the parent's overprotectiveness communicates a lack of confidence in the child's ability to cope, thus reinforcing the child's feelings of inadequacy.
4. The failure of an indifferent or detached parent to provide adequate guidance for a child's development. Although the child is not necessarily rejected, neither is he adequately supported in mastering essential competencies and in gaining a positive self-concept. Repeated experiences of failure, stemming from poor learning skills, may lead to subsequent patterns of anxiety or withdrawal in the face of "threatening" situations.

A third disorder is Posttraumatic Stress Disorder (PTSD). It is when the cause of the stress is unusually severe (that is, outside the realm of typical human experience) and is psychologically traumatic. Examples include a life-threatening situation (such as being in a car accident), the destruction of one's home, seeing another person mutilated or killed, or being the victim of physical violence. PTSD is categorized as an anxiety disorder and there are feelings of fear and apprehension involved (Carson, 1992). Posttraumatic stress disorder includes the following symptoms:

1. The child persistently re-experiences the traumatic event - she may have intrusive, recurring thoughts or repetitive nightmares about the event.
2. The child persistently avoids stimuli associated with the trauma. For example, she tries to avoid activities related to the incident or blocks out the memory of certain aspects of the experience. Situations that recall the traumatic experience provoke anxiety.
3. The child may experience persistent symptoms of increased arousal, such as chronic tension and irritability, often accompanied by insomnia and the inability to tolerate noise.
4. The child may experience impaired concentration and memory.
5. The child may experience feelings of depression. In some cases, she may withdraw from social contact.

Several investigators of child abuse believe that residual symptoms of sexual abuse can be characterized as a type of posttraumatic stress disorder because the symptoms experienced are similar; for example, nightmares, flashbacks, sleep problems, and feelings of estrangement. According to Carson (1992), in child abuse cases 20 to 40 percent of the children have been seriously injured. Although children and adolescents of all ages are physically abused, the most frequent cases involve children under 3 years of age. Some evidence suggests that boys are more often abused than girls are.

Posttraumatic dreams may be a form of remembering, a repetition of the past (Hunt, 1986). Research has shown an increased dream recall and more nightmare distress among trauma victims (Punamaki, 1999). Dreaming is generally a response to the experiences of the previous day. However, among trauma victims, the dreaming process incorporates intrusion of painful memories and overwhelming negative feelings.

According to Siegel (1996), nightmares are a common feature of PTSD. The presence of nightmares may be a sign of positive adaptation showing that the dreamer can tolerate the remembering of the upsetting event as opposed to avoiding and denying them. Dreams involving conflict and struggle may indicate that progress is occurring in the resolution of the conflict. Frightening dreams may signal a long-delayed release of confrontation with the traumatic emotions or a stirring of anxieties from a more recent event. Having nightmares after a traumatic event often reflects a normal psychic healing process.

Siegel (1996) explains how posttraumatic nightmares are different from normal nightmares:
1. PTSD nightmares are more emotionally intrusive and anxiety provoking.
2. Blank or content-less nightmares may occur before the dreamer can tolerate any recall of the affects connected to the trauma.
3. They may be repetitive and unchanging nightmares with minimal adaptive response to threats arising in the dream.

4. PTSD nightmares consistently repeat some aspects of the trauma but with some elements changed or missing.
5. Encapsulation: Like a psychological abscess, intolerable emotions and conflicts linked to the trauma continue to infect the psyche but are walled off from consciousness, yet persist in dreams.
6. Fading: As a trauma is resolved, there is less fixation on the trauma as the major theme in dreams and trauma-related conflicts are mixed with current issues and challenges.

According to studies done by Punamaki (1999), some traumatized children who felt fearful, angry, and worried in the evening had compensatory dreams that had happy recreation themes. Compensatory dreams provide the dreamer with consolation and relief from a painful reality by incorporating pleasant thoughts and feelings. Morning moods often mirror the feelings in the dream.

Depression. Depression can be a cause of nightmares. It can attack children as young as four or five as well as teens. The symptoms of depression are different in children than they are in adults. They can include irritability, rage, and physical complaints such as stomachaches, headaches, and dizziness. There may also be bedwetting, aggressive behavior and nightmares. Stone (1995) describes a few of the main categories of depression in children:

Manic Depression is also known as bipolar I and bipolar II, and it is usually an inherited disease. Manic depression cycles between very low depressive periods coupled with manic highs. Usually behavior during manic high periods includes high excitability, rapid speech, hyperactivity and fearless behavior (such as the belief that one can fly like Superman). Some bipolar patients can actually hear voices telling them what to do. Children as young as five have been diagnosed with manic depression. There is no known cure but it can be controlled with medication.

Major Depression is another category, but it is not common among children. However, it is possible that a teen may experience this form. This type of depression is the result of an imbalance in brain chemicals, and the most common successful treatment involves the use of antidepressant medication. Teens who experience major depression will be focused on themselves and their problems. They will be moody, uncommunicative, either overeating or not eating, and they will seek relief from their emotional pain. This is when most teens will turn to using drugs or alcohol.

Dysthymia is another category of depression. It means "low-grade" depression. The symptoms are not as pronounced as they are with major or manic depression. If the child is having difficulty staying focused in school, is moody, or complains a lot about physical symptoms then he may have dysthymia. Although dysthymia can be cured with antidepressant medication, it can also be treated nutritionally. Some foods which are known to help lift mild depression include brown rice, fish, eggs, dairy products, soya beans, wheatgerm and whole-grains (Edgson & Marber, 1999).

Reactive Depression is a final category, and it is what most children will experience. This depression occurs in response to a loss, such as the divorce or separation of parents, being placed in new surroundings, attending a new school, etc. This depression does not usually require medical treatment.

Medication. Certain medications (See Appendix A) can produce or bring out severe nightmare: for example beta-blockers, antidepressants, and medication used for hypertension. If a person with little or no history of nightmares suddenly begins to experience them, it is a good idea to check out the possibility that medication is the root of the nightmare. Often, simply changing the medicine can solve the problem (Hartmann, 1987).

Rapid withdrawal from some drugs can cause nightmares. For example, many medications (especially painkillers) suppress dreaming. As pain medication is reduced, the brain experiences what is called "REM rebound." This phenomenon is a state of intense, vivid, often terrifying dreams. It is the natural outcome of having had dreams suppressed for several days. The brain needs to compensate for its dream inhibition (Garfield, 1991).

What To Do If Your Child Is Having A Nightmare

If your child is having a nightmare Dr. John Pearce (1999) suggests the following steps:
- Go in and reassure your child with your familiar bedtime phrase [such as "good night, sleep tight"]. Reassure the child that everything is all right. Tuck the child in gently and leave the room as soon as possible.
- Keep a chart. Is your child having nightmares for a particular reason? Is the child worried about school or another child? Is there a pattern to the night-mares?
- Repeated nightmares can often be controlled. For example, if the dream in-volves a monster chasing your child, work out a plan with the child to deal with the monster. You can do this while the child is still in bed. For example, you can suggest that the child can make the monster fall down a hole or get trapped in a cage [see the section on Nightmare Help for other options].
- In the morning, ask older children if they want to tell you about the nightmare.

If your child is having a night terror Dr. Pearce suggests the following steps:

- Don't wake the child. It's almost impossible to do and will upset both of you.
- Wait next to the child patiently. The terror will soon pass. It usually only lasts a few minutes, but it could last up to 30 minutes.

- After it's over, tuck the child in quietly and say your familiar bedtime phrase to reassure the child.
- Keep a chart. If the terrors happen regularly, wake the child just before it's about to start so you interrupt the sleep cycle. Then coax the child back to sleep again. If it continues, see your doctor.
- As stated earlier, the child won't remember the night terror in the morning. So don't worry too much.

Young children may have trouble distinguishing between what is real and what is not in a dream. This could cause some concern for the child. As a result they may ask questions following a nightmare in order to reassure themselves. Pitcher & Prelinger (1963) were presented with these questions during their studies: Can witches really turn children into gingerbread? Can magic wands really kill? Can you kill a ghost? Do bullets hurt? Can statues become real? Can you take the eyes of a real man and put them in a clay man? Do crosses and stars that talk have someone inside of them?

Recurring Nightmares

According to Siegel & Bulkeley (1998), recurring nightmares are often a warning of lingering psychological conflicts. For example, children of divorce frequently dream that their parents have reunited; abuse survivors are often the victims of perpetrators of violence in their dreams; and adopted children intermittently dream of their birth parents.

Changes within the recurring dreams may signal the onset of resolving a psychological impasse. For example, a survivor of child abuse who was making a therapeutic breakthrough in her emotional recovery dreamed of triumphing over a shadowy, hostile figure that had threatened and chased her in innumerable prior nightmares.

Siegel & Bulkeley present three stages of resolution that can be identified in children's nightmares:
- Threat: in the dream, a main character is threatened and unable to mount any defense. For example, he may be paralyzed while trying to flee the jaws of a hungry ghost imprisoned by aliens.
- Struggle: Attempts to confront the nightmare adversary are partially successful in fending off danger. An example would be temporarily escaping a robber with a knife and trying to dial the phone for help.
- Resolution: The nightmare enemy, opponent, or oppressor is vanquished and the threatening creatures are put in cages, slain, or held at bay with magic wands, or otherwise disarmed.

In some cases, children spontaneously resolve a recurring nightmare as the formerly distressing situations, which caused the nightmares, get worked out in the child's real life. A crucial factor in understanding repetitive dreams is looking at the degree of resolution or mastery in the dream. As children mature emotionally and intellectually, they gain increasing control over their childhood fears and feel more confident in their ability to solve problems and handle situations independently. This gradually increasing sense of control is reflected not only in waking achievements but in their dream life (Siegel & Bulkeley, 1998).

Chapter 6
What Is Your Child Dreaming?

The contents of children's dreams will reflect the child's range of experience and the particular age in terms of the physical world (society). The child will experience pleasures and pain, gratification and frustration, enhancement and oppression, enthusiasm and fear, and opportunity and limitations. The child's life will involve interpersonal relationships, moralistic restriction and individual expression (Pitcher & Prelinger, 1963).

<u>Aggression In Dreams</u>

One of the most common types of aggression dream involves the dreamer being pursued and/or attacked. This type of dream could represent the dreamer's self-conception as a weak, passive, inferior, or helpless person at the time the dream appeared. Such dreams may also represent anxieties concerning the harmful intentions of others towards the dreamer, but in some cases the person in the attacking role represents a projected and disowned part of the dreamer's personality (Van de Castle, 1994).

Potential destruction and aggression in dreams may express not only aggressive impulses on the part of the child, or a concern with suffering physical harm, but also with a central preoccupation with the possible loss of a secure sense of self (Pitcher & Prelinger, 1963). It is sometimes difficult to realize how vivid and omnipresent such concerns are to a young child.

Studies done by Foulkes (1978) show that children of all ages, both boys and girls, rarely initiate aggressive acts in their dreams, instead other dream characters initiate them. His studies also showed that the children were rarely the recipients of the aggressive acts of others in the dreams, but rather an observer of the action.

Aggressive impulses that have been stifled in waking life, but are still breeding resentment in the depths of the unconscious, will often show up in dreams. Someone else may seem to be the aggressor, while the dreamer appears to be the victim or innocent bystander, isolated from the violence or even appalled by it. Yet the dream may still be revealing something about the dreamer's underlying aggression, how the dreamer proposes to handle these impulses, and the possible consequences (Chetwynd, 1980).

Death In Dreams

In many cases it is difficult for a child to separate the theme of death from that of aggression. Death is a form of aggression, in most cases, which at least temporarily puts people out of circulation. Death is often a young child's way of stopping something or winning. Characters that have been burned, devoured, run over or shot are often believed to be dead. But death is by no means final for a child - it is a stunning rather than a knockout blow. Half the time the "dead" character comes back into action again (Pitcher & Prelinger, 1963).

Dreaming of oneself as dead could mean a fear of life and retreating from it. The dead have no more fears. It may come from a feeling of incompetence, helplessness, disorientation, or estrangement (Chetwynd, 1980). Someone who is pretending to be dying could mean that the dreamer is pretending an unawareness of what is going on in waking life (Pitcher & Prelinger, 1963). A child that dreams she is dead may be feeling neglected or abandoned in waking life. There may be a fear of death, especially if someone the child knows has recently died.

Dreaming that a known person has died may represent some aspect of the dreamer - they may share a common characteristic or behavior. For example, a child may dream that a playmate is hit by a car while riding his bike in the street. The child having the dream may also ride his bike in the street and see the dream as a warning. Dreaming that a loved one has died may show a hidden resentment or emotion (Delaney, 1997). For example, a girl has a major fight with her brother and then dreams that the brother is dead. Dreaming that a parent has died may represent that the child has a fear of losing the parent or of being separated in some way, such as after a divorce.

Animals in Dreams

Children dream of animals more than adults do. Animals are pervasive in a child's experience. Even a child without pets or unfamiliar with other types of animals is still exposed to a high dosage of animals through television, movies, picture books, and stories. Garfield (1984) believes that children perceive animals as having a freedom denied to them. Animals don't have to control their hunger or their bowels or their sexual feelings, as parents insist children do. Sometimes animals can successfully defy parental authority in ways rarely available to children. Vicariously, the child triumphs.

In many children's dreams, animals represent the main characters. As such, the animal clearly becomes the carrier of the child's own wishes, worries, and concerns. The choice of animals as personal representatives of the child can be interpreted in terms of projection, of displacement, or of symbolism. These three processes could represent defensive operations by means of which the dreamer having wishes, worries, and concerns is disguised (Pitcher & Prelinger, 1963).

Animals can also represent unconscious ideas that are being made possible through the dreams. For example, if the child dreamed of an angry lion, it's possible that the child was angry at the time of the dream. Foulkes (1982) describes this as a convenient fill-in for the self-representation when the child's cognitive immaturity makes it impossible for him to construct a more literal self-approximation.

Animals in children's dreams often have human characteristics. They will talk and walk on two legs. Ferocious wild animals may become friendly and will often be seen as toys. They may perform tasks, for example, a bear was washing dishes. The animal may actually *be* the child: the little horse got in trouble for waking up his baby brother (Pitcher & Prelinger, 1963).

On the other hand, domestic animals (such as cats and dogs) may become ferocious, intent on biting or killing a victim (usually the dreamer). These animals may also represent the child. They may serve as a convenient representative of the child's consciously unaccepted wishes to harm and destroy or of angers and disappointments. The child's "bad" unconscious wishes can be expressed through such indirect means since they are attributed to somebody else, and in particular to beings, which are generally defined as dangerous and bad.

After having a nightmare, three-year-old Trey talks about killing his pets. Even though he had always treated his pets with love he says, "If I had a gun I'd shoot that dog. And I'd shoot that lizard. Then I'd shoot lions." Had he been dreaming about being attacked by animals or was it easier to take out his aggression on the animals instead of the person he was angry at in waking life?

If the attacker in a dream is an animal, some clues may be found about its presence by asking what attributes of the animal can be associated with the dreamer. For example, does the animal bite, strangle or stomp its victim? Does the dreamer or someone they know act this way in waking life (Van de Castle, 1994)? Studies have shown that many of the children who had dreams of aggressive animals were themselves vigorous, assertive, and aggressive in their waking lives (Foulkes, 1982). Animal dreams are associated with more emotional intensity than non-animal dreams and they decrease with increasing age (Van de Castle, 1966).

Garfield (1984) says people tend to feature a limited number of animals in their dreams that have personal significance. This choice seems to begin in childhood. Some people's dreams will be full of horses and dogs, and someone else will dream of cats and birds. Early in life the animals are chosen that portray characteristics with which the child identifies. And although the emphasis may shift from time to time, the person remains relatively loyal to them.

We dream more often of animals well known to us such as pets, past and present. We also dream of animals we are familiar with from favorite stories, television shows, and movies. Thoughts and fantasies knit themselves together from the yarn of our waking hours and so do our dreams. A fond acquaintance with an actual animal and with an emotional association with a fictional one can make an appropriate dream symbol that can express a need in the dreamer (Garfield, 1984).

Garfield continues, saying that by examining the animals in children's dreams and observing the role they play can help parents to understand the child better. Any character (animal or human) that recurs often in a child's dream does so because of the dreamer's emotional involvement - love or hate - with them. Besides knowing what animal frequents the child's dreams, the parent also needs to know what the animal signifies to the child. Garfield gives several methods for discovering this significance:
- Ask the child how she would describe the animal (appearing in the dream) to a child who is younger and has never seen or heard about one. Even if the animal is negative, the answer will help understand its role better.
- Ask the child, "If you were an animal, what kind would you *most* want to be?" When a reply is made ask "Why?" Next, ask the question "If you were an animal, what kind would you *least* like to be?" and "Why?"
- Ask the child, "If you were a [the animal appearing in the dream] would you like it?" "Why?" or "Why not?"

Emotions in Dreams

Sometimes our dreams exaggerate feelings and emotions just to wake us up and give us solutions to our real life problems (Wiseman, 1989). Exploring the feelings that arise in a dream will help the parent to understand what the child is experiencing in waking life.

Anger. According to Campbell (1999), children need help in identifying and labeling their feelings. A primary reason for this is that children often show anger when they are actually experiencing other feelings such as rejection, stress, loneliness, inadequacy, or weakness. The sooner a child can learn to tell the difference between anger and other feelings, the sooner the child will be able to express himself in better ways.

Campbell continues, stating that aggression is one of the most common immature expressions of anger. Some children find it difficult to monitor their own aggressive impulses. One moment they are playing happily, the next they are lashing out at someone who has upset them. Left unchecked, aggressive behavior can cause them to be shunned by their peers, resulting in feelings of rejection and then more anger. The child may become depressed because of his feeling of being out of control. The earlier children are shown how to handle their anger and channel their aggressive impulses, the sooner the downward spiral can be halted (Spurr, 1999).

Ventilation. Ventilation is a verbal expression of anger. It differs from verbal aggression in that its intent is not to bring harm to another person, but simply to get rid of one's anger. This type of behavior may range from loud, angry screaming to muttered expletives, from complaining and arguing to hysterical tirades. Anger comes out in two different ways, verbally or behaviorally, and if the child is expressing anger verbally, he is probably not expressing it behaviorally, as in aggression or passive aggression. Most children employ verbal expressions of anger. The more parents prevent this expression, by telling children to "Shut up!" or "Don't talk like that!" the more the anger will come out behaviorally (Campbell, 1999). Working with a child and his dreams is a safe way of exploring anger.

Depression. Studies have shown that the depressed dreamer often portrays himself as the recipient of painful experiences in dreams. There is also low self-regard and high self-criticism and self-blame (Cartwright, Lloyd, Knight, & Trenholme, 1984). For a person who is depressed the dreams are frequently longer than normal, are more dreamlike in quality, and will express more negative content.

Anxiety. According to Foulkes (1978), many children experience dreams that produce anxiety, in which a REM mental drama gets "out of hand." These dreams occur in proportion to the child's difficulties in managing his waking life. The studies show that these anxiety dreams are not typical of any developmental stage, and that the capacity to generate unpleasant as well as pleasant dream scenarios actually increases in step with waking cognitive development.

Child Acting Out Dream With Day Time Actions

For children and young adolescents, almost all mental activity is unconscious. The parent must deduce from their behavior what is going on (Peck, 1998). Some day time actions can be the result of the child acting out his dreams.

According to Wiseman (1989), very young children may not understand that they have dreamed. For them, there is no distinction between a dream image and reality. They may be convinced that the dream images are real. For example, a child may dream that there is a monster in the room. Parents can show the child that there is no monster, but no amount of searching the bedroom will make the child feel safe enough to go back to sleep. What's to keep the monster from coming back? Piaget (1963) found that very young children typically believe that their dreams are actually *in* the room or *in* the bed.

Children sometimes feel guilty about what has happened in their dreams. For example, if a child dreams that her parents got a divorce, she may feel responsible, as if she were to blame. This is called magical thinking. A child needs to know that dreaming about something doesn't make it happen (Wiseman, 1989).

According to Van de Castle (1994), the amount of effort we expend in our dreams may have a direct bearing upon how tired or refreshed we are in the morning, and our dream moods may carry over into our morning moods. If we are active in our dreams, climbing mountains or struggling to figure out a difficult mental problem, we will probably wake up feeling tired. This is more likely if our strenuous efforts fail to achieve success. If we reach our desired goal, getting to the top of the mountain or solving an intellectual task, the elation accompanying the accomplishment may override the sense of fatigue that would ordinarily be associated with the dreamed-of exertion.

Generally, a child dreaming of threatening strangers and bizarre animals will feel more fearful in the morning. On the other hand, children having happy, recreational dreams will be feeling happy in the morning (Punamaki, 1999). Children who experience anger, depression or anxiety in their dreams will wake up mirroring these feelings. Children who experience joy, love, and excitement in their dreams will wake up with similar feelings.

Hints Of A Personal Reality

It is often better to let go of our emotions than to keep them under tight reins. Dreams are by and large outside of conscious control, revealing aspects of the dreamer that may not be noticed in waking life. The dreamer may be perplexed about what a dream means, but asking certain questions may enlighten him:
- Why did I have this dream?
- What does this dream mean?
- Why does this dream bother me?

Dreams provide hints of a personal reality typically unknown - a personal reality which contrasts with everyday self-perception. Somewhere within dreams there may be hidden aspects of the deeper self (Gackenbach & Bosveld, 1989).

Nine-year-old David was allergic to animals. Whenever he petted a cat his eyes and sinuses swelled up and he couldn't breathe. He had a dream in which a cat was rubbing itself over him. After awakening, he experienced a full-blown allergy attack. Was the dream an indication of an upcoming attack or did the dream itself cause it (Van de Castle, 1994)? Five-year-old Karen, also allergic to animals, wakes in the middle of the night in the midst of a full-blown asthma attack. Is she dreaming of an animal?

Four-year-old Suzy, chatting away happily, was riding down the road with her grandmother. As they passed a creek, Suzy looked at it and suddenly said, "And then Uncle Eddie turned into a monster, then he turned back into Uncle Eddie." Suzy then went on to name each man in her life saying they also turned into a monster. Was Suzy talking about an unpleasant experience or was she reporting a dream?

What Are Children Dreaming About?

Children's dream reports not only grow longer as the children age, they also shift in arrangement. At first, their dreams are single scenes, such as "I was in a cave." Later, the dream description is more like a camera left running: several scenes are strung together but do not necessarily seem to be related. Still later, the dream takes on an edited quality: a theme appears to run through the scenes; they are not simply sequential. Some dream scenes are equivalent to zoom shots on the screen, close-ups, or aerial views, all relating to the story under way. Older children have more organized dreams (Garfield, 1984).

Newborn to 3 years. Do babies dream? REM sleep is described as a process for "programming" the brain. This programming system is homeostatic, organizing and storing memories (perceptual, cognitive, and behavioral programs). The newborn needs more REM time than adults do to develop the central nervous system. Slow brain wave pattern sleep does not occur until the central nervous system has acquired a certain amount of maturity. Prematurely born infants spend about 80 percent of their sleeping time in the REM state. The full-term baby spends about 50 percent of his time dreaming, the five-week-old infant about 40 percent, and the three-year-old about 30 percent (Krippner & Hughes, 1970).

If you watch an infant sleep you will be able to see the movement of her eyes under her closed lids as she dreams. It's probable that at 6 months of age, the child is not really seeing images in dreams but is reacting to the feelings the dreams produce. These feelings could be internal such as feeling abandoned (Erikson, 1959), or external such as feeling hungry, cold, or sick. Although many young children don't really have a concept of what a dream is, there are some children that experience a spontaneous nightmare and non-nightmare dream recall (Piaget, 1962).

<u>3 to 5 years.</u> Dream reporting at this age is usually very brief and often static in quality, since dream recall is usually not very good. Children usually dream of nuclear family members and known persons. They more often dream of animals, especially barnyard animals. Presumably this restriction of dream characterization to the familiar and the significant reflects not only the limited perspectives of the child's waking world but also the difficulty in being able to reconstruct that world symbolically (Foulkes, 1977).

It's very common at this age for children to have a lot of fatigue or sleep themes in their dreams. For example: the boy was sleeping in the window of a barbershop; he was sleeping atop a fire engine; he was sleeping in a banana tree; he was sleeping in an unfamiliar house. These types of dreams may suggest that the sleeper is highly susceptible to having his thoughts influenced by the state of his body. This ties in with the preoperational stage of thinking (Foulkes, 1982).

Hunger dreams are often common at this age. However, the children more likely will be dreaming that *other* people are eating or doing things related to food. For example: the girl's mother was baking cookies; the boy was watching his father eat a hamburger; the girl went grocery shopping with her mother (Garfield, 1984).

Dream settings at this age, when children are able to construct (or report) them are generally of highly familiar places. Usually dreams are in their home settings. Socially inexperienced children may simply not have any knowledge of other indoor settings. Outdoor dreams seem to have vague settings. Children are likely to just say, "I was outside." Then when asked where "outside" really is, they respond, "Just outside."

Activities in dreams at this age include more motor activity than sensory, meaning there is more physical activity than feelings. Other dream characters mainly perform the activities. In testing done by David Foulkes (1982), it was shown that children who were judged high in make-believe or pretend behavior had more motor activity in their dreams.

According to Foulkes, feeling states in dream characters for the 3 to 5 year-olds are little if any. Dream characters rarely think anything in the dreams, and they rarely have any feelings. This isn't surprising since the child's psychological perspective isn't well developed yet. Children this age are in the preoperational stage of ego development. For example, they may not understand what the word "feeling" means (what was the boy feeling?). They can usually understand how the dream makes them feel as they are telling it, but not how they actually felt during the dream.

Foulkes' studies further show that it is not only what a child experiences or

84

what interests the child, but also how adequately a child can reconstruct reality symbolically that determines his dream content. Also a child of this age may have trouble describing a dream, both visually and linguistically. Not only how one *sees* the world, but also how one is able to *think* about it will determine dream content. Studies done by Garfield show that little girls this age will dream of their dolls, but no other toys are mentioned in the dreams of either sex (1984).

5 to 7 years. At this age there is more extensive dream content than at earlier ages. Children are now in transition from the preoperational stage of cognition to the operational stage of thinking. In this transition, egocentrism declines as rational rules begin to replace self-references as dominant forces in thought organization. With this decentering from momentary mood states or circumstances of the self, there is increasing comprehension of the realm of the not-self, of both the material and the social worlds lying outside the child's own skin (Foulkes, 1982).

Dream reporting is longer at this age. Dreams may have become longer, but more likely the child's language ability has increased. Children this age are generally in primary school where their verbal skills are improving, making it easier for them to describe their dreams. There is also an increase in social interaction and physical movement in dreams at this age. Children are now able to construct reasonably well-defined characters and settings that transcend the familiar.

By ages 5 to 7 children's dreams are beginning to be *stories* rather than static descriptions. Dreams now begin to construct a mini-world, closely modeled on the real one, in which characters perform activities, pursue goals, and even realize the consequences of their actions. The activities are recognizably like, but not identical to, activities the child performs or knows about in waking life.

Studies done by Foulkes also show that family members appear considerably but not significantly more often in the dreams of children ages 5 to 7 than at 3 to 5. The nuclear family members were most often portrayed, while extended family (such as aunts, uncles, grandparents, etc.) seldom appeared. The studies also show that, if one family member is present in the dream, the other family members generally seem to be present as well. In the dreaming child's mind, the basic choice seems to be "family" vs. "not," with little discrimination made among family members. Children do not seem to draw distinctions between male and female family members. Family is family, a unit.

At this age, there is a significant increase in dream activities. Motives and interpersonal outcomes are largely limited to those centered about other characters than the dreamer himself, especially for boys. The child's dreams are about things that are happening around him, but in which he is not a major actor.

Animals in dreams decrease slightly. The types of animals change; there

85

are less barnyard animals and wild animals and more pets. Foulkes (1982) suggests that pets are animals that the child can control or manage, thereby representing the real-life requirement of increased impulse control. As a person becomes more capable of dealing with the "wildness" within himself, less of it appears in the shape of animals in his dreams.

At this age, the male and female will start to have slightly different dream themes. Girls claim to have more happy dreams, and they start taking a more active role in them. Animals start to be replaced by familial characters. Girls dream more of home settings. On the other hand, boys often begin to take a more passive role. Dream settings are more often outdoors, and there is a higher incidence of male strangers. There is an increase in animal characters in boys' dreams and a low incidence of family members and home settings. The boys' dreams now seem to be occupied with conflict. While there is little hostility, there seems to be a parallel growth of coping resources, on the one hand, with those of feeling and impulse on the other (Foulkes, 1977).

There is now less confusion on the child's part between *seeing* a dream and seeing *in* a dream. There are more motor acts and self-involvement in dreams. Both sensory and motor acts ascribed to the dreamer are associated with high language quality. This suggests the possibility that grammatical competence plays some role in the enhanced self-participation in the dreams of 5- to 7-year-olds. Foulkes states that the child's participation in his dreams will depend on his achievement of linguistic competence and/or operationality.

Children at this age still generally don't assign feeling states to their dream characters although they can say how the dream makes them feel after waking. For example: I feel happy, or the dream scares me. There is also an increase in social themes as the child himself has increased social activity in waking life. Only about one in four dreams include aggression, and the dreamer is rarely the initiator or recipient (Foulkes, 1982).

7 to 9 years. At this age there is a significant increase in dream reporting. This suggests a continuous increase in attention, memory, vocabulary, and so forth, showing a shift in attaining operational reasoning. This also shows that there are underlying changes in the actual experiencing of dreams.

At this age there is an increase of the children themselves being characters in their dreams. They now move about within the dream, they experience drive-states, and can both initiate and interact with other dream characters. Dream characters now have thoughts and feelings. There is an increase in pro-social and pleasurable dream sequences. It is a socialized self who is newly being inserted into a socialized dream world, says Foulkes (1982).

Frequently at this age there are themes of growth. The boy often acts like a "big guy" having very adventurous dreams. There are also male themes, such as war and hunting. There may also be dreams pertaining to the pitfalls that occur along this path of growth. For example: his new fishing pole was too big for him to use; he was climbing through the branches of a tree and fell out, hitting the ground; the chain on the bicycle he was riding fell off; he was flying a plane but it crashed.

Boys now dream of family members and known males more often than of animal characters. At this age there is a high number of dreams with father oriented activities. The father is often seen as a role model and as a protector. While both parental figures are common the mother figure is more likely to be a supporting player, while the father's masculine competence serves as a central focus for modeling and identification. Competition dreams are also common. For example: competition with father, competition with siblings, competition with peers, and so forth. These types of dreams suggest the struggle to achieve adult status (Foulkes, 1967).

Girl's dreams frequently occur more often in the home setting. Dream activity usually takes place in the girl's own home: the kitchen, her bedroom, the living room, the attic or the cellar. In their dreams, most girls are homebodies. Settings in a dream reflect the interests, tastes, and resources of the people who inhabit them. Familiar places, especially the dreamer's home and the homes of friends and other family members, occur more often in the majority of girl's dreams (Garfield, 1984).

School-related themes are rare for boys at this age, despite the increasing hours they spend in academic pursuit. This may suggest that the major concern of the preadolescent boy is the complex developmental task of becoming grown-up, competent, and masculine. Girls occasionally have school-related themes, perhaps showing that school is more involving for the girls than for the boys. According to Garfield (1984), dreams about school-related subjects may occur most often for the children who are having some type of difficulty with school in waking life.

Both boys and girls have an increase of incidences with adult male strangers, perhaps to meet in different ways their separate needs in sex-role socialization: to have grown-up role models, and to have models to play one's grown-up role opposite. Boys have twice as many men in their dreams than women. Girls, however, have an equal amount of men and women. At this age, boys have fewer people altogether in their dreams than the girls do. This often continues throughout adulthood.

9 to 11 years. Dreams at this age don't change very much from the 7 to 9 year-old dreams. There seems to be a continuity. Foulkes (1982) explains that most children have already accomplished dream development by the age of 9.

There is little room left for major change in the form of dream content until new problems of psychosocial adaptation, and the new possibilities of abstract thinking associated with adolescence, begins. On the other hand, for dreams as for other aspects of psychological development, middle childhood and preadolescence are periods more of consolidation and continuity than of cataclysmic change.

At this age, girls generally dream more often of parental figures than at earlier ages. For both boys and girls, those with less than optimal parenting dream more often of parents and other family members. Paternal authoritarianism is associated with dreaming of male family members, and maternal authoritarianism with dreaming of female members. Such attributes no doubt make parents more salient figures in children's lives, as well as contributing to a closeness, if not cohesiveness, in family relationships more generally.

Boys continue to have more outdoor and adventurous dreams than the girls do. There are frequently dreams of masculine recreation (such as hunting and fishing) and sports. Foulkes (1967) refers to this as a rehearsal of the male adult role. Sometimes the boy is participating in the action, and other times he is just a passive observer, such as sitting in the bleachers during a baseball game.

Children now have an increase in self-participation in their dreams. The self-character also usually becomes the prominent role in the dream. Most children this age now have the ability to picture a dream through their "own" (i.e. the self-character's) eyes. The self-character has an increase of speaking in the dreams now. Studies done by Foulkes, show that children with a high verbal I.Q. will have a higher frequency of verbalization in their dreams. Children who scored high in performance skills had a higher frequency of physical activities in their dreams.

Children's dream contents now show coherently individual differences in personal style. This self-revelatory aspect of dreaming will reflect the child's personality and the dreams will represent her typical waking behaviors, interests and attitudes. Children are now better able to express primary emotions in themselves and to have other dream characters express emotions in dreams. Anger seems to be the most prominent emotion in dreams at this age, followed by anxiety and fear (Foulkes, 1982).

11 to 13 years. The changes in children's dreams will reflect their personal growth and social development. According to Foulkes (1982), at this age, children's dreams less often contain family members, particularly female family members, including the mother. Dreams are now more about the children's peers, although girls dream more about their female peers than the boys do of their male peers.

Children also dream less of the home setting and more often about unfamiliar residential settings and recreational environments. As children's waking lives become increasingly symbolic, so will their dream worlds. The extra-familial world is being explored with increasing confidence and competence. There is an effective integration of the self with others, and dream activities are increasingly verbal-symbolic in nature.

Foulkes's studies also show that late preadolescence is usually associated with an early integration of cognitive functions. It is a period of organization and consolidation that will guide the child through the flux of adolescence toward a second and more mature structuring of the self. By the ages of 11 to 13, children's dreams are consistent with the preadolescent attainment of self-mastery and self-control. By this age the children's dreams are generally as well organized and as well controlled as they ever have been or ever will be.

For characters other than the self-character there is now an increase in psychological acts, such as seeing, sensing, and talking in the dream. The self-character begins to have more physical behaviors, such as manipulating and moving. Girls, more than boys, report more pleasant dreams than at earlier ages (Foulkes, 1978). However, the feeling states in dreams seem to decrease slightly. Social apprehension rather than the primitive anxiety that is felt in younger children usually cause fear that is felt in dreams.

<u>Adolescence to adult.</u> Dreaming for the adolescent, or young adult, will generally be the same as adult dreaming. The contents will contain the actions and concerns of waking life. Teenagers are usually in school, getting their first job, first car, and first bank account. There is now a stronger search for identity as the teenager gets to know herself, her ideals, her abilities, talents, and her morality. Relationships now turn from same-sex peers to opposite-sex unions.

Holloway (2001) writes that in the teen years there are frequent dreams about romantic relationships. During these years, the dreams are kind of a loves-me, loves-me-not story line that continues into adulthood. The goal of these dreams seems to be to recognize subtle cues of attraction, figure out how to win love and pleasure, and to understand sexual feelings.

Adolescents have a need for acceptance and validation of their decisions. Teenagers are in the process of deciding what is okay, desirable, or possible, and what will hold them back, reflect badly on them, or make them appear less grown up. Dream themes of killing someone or something or of burying something can reflect these concerns. The dead or buried dream image represents an undesirable aspect of the dreamer that he wishes to disown. There is often a fear of discovery caused by the desire to conceal (or erase) the existence of the quality of the self that is being set aside. This type of dream also symbolizes the end of one era and the beginning of the next.

During teen years, both boys and girls begin to dream regularly of hanging out with celebrities. The teen will usually feel a connection with a particular star, or even the entire cast of a television program. She will then dream repeatedly of being among the close circle of people surrounding the star or of being a member of the cast. The basic recurring element of these dreams is that of being a part of a group of talented, admired people. The focus is on group solidarity, creative projects, and supporting the movies, music, or activities for which the celebrities are famous.

These dreams seem to serve a number of purposes. They allow the teen to be a part of an interesting, tight group and to have a sense of playing an important role within the group. They also give the dreamer a vivid sense of participating in an ensemble effort, including the necessity to gauge when to support the needs of the personalities involved, and when to stringently pursue artistic goals. Finally, these dreams seem to provide a practice ground in which unique abilities fit with collective goals, and talents find new channels for expression (Holloway, 2001).

Chapter 7
Working With Children and Their Dreams

Children are prolific dreamers. They are less inhibited than adults are and less concerned about concealing anything unpleasant in their dreams. When adults dream of something that makes them feel uncomfortable, they frequently dismiss the dream on waking, frightened to acknowledge their discomfort and the possible causes of it in their waking life. Although children are in the process of developing such subconscious protective mechanisms, they are much more likely to be eager to share their dream experiences with their parents. On the other hand, they may have difficulty communicating their dream experiences through lack of understanding of particular images or the emotions aroused by them or through insufficient vocabulary to describe their dreams adequately. Or they may simply feel that their parents are too busy to spend time listening to them as they recount their dreams (Spurr, 1999).

Parents should create dream awareness in their children. This can be a gradual process. It can begin by the parent relating a dream of her own. Children any age will find this interesting. They will wonder at the strange occurrences that went on. If they have never really been aware of dreaming before, they may be fascinated and ask numerous questions about the dream. Parents should fill in the details at the level the children will understand.

Next, if the children are very young, ask them if they have ever had a dream. If the child is older, she may have already related some, especially nightmares. Ask the child to tell you about any dreams she may remember. Allow the communication to develop slowly. Once the child is used to talking about her dreams and listening to her parents talk about theirs, start to encourage her positively to dream. At bedtime talk to her about all the wonderful possibilities that exist in dreamland (Spurr, 1999).

Help children understand the three levels of dream exploration: (a) the effect of their body condition and the environment on their dreams; (b) the effect of their feelings on dreams - problems and pleasures of the moment and from the past; and (c) how their dreams can motivate and inspire them just as they have many famous dreamers (Garfield, 1984). Encourage the children to create artwork based on their dreams.

Dreamwork is the process of recalling, recording, and finding the meaning and value of a dream. The dreamer is always the final authority on what the dream means. Others can offer insight and suggestions, but since each dream is so personal and unique only the dreamer can fully understand and know what the final meaning of the dream will be. Usually there will be an "aha" feeling of recognition when the meaning of the dream has been revealed, although this probably doesn't happen with little children.

Dream Recall

Learning to remember dreams requires an active stance during the day. Motivation is a huge factor in remembering. Therefore, there should be the intention to pay attention to one's dreams. It is rare that an entire dream will be recalled, and this can cause some feelings of frustration. However, usually the entire dream is not needed in order to understand the meaning of the dream. Henry Reed (1973) lists the following categories of dream recall:
1. *Indistinct* refers to the vague recall of dream residue or the awareness of dreaming without the ability to recall any content.
2. *Fragmentary* refers to minimal recall of the narrative itself, which conveys some sense of the dream but which lacks flux or transitions.
3. *Partial* refers to the incomplete recall of a dream, which includes at least one clear example of a transition to indicate the flow of the narrative. However, the dreamer feels there are gaps in his memory of the dream.
4. *Whole* refers to the fairly complete recall of a dream with no gaps to indicate loss of memory.

There are many ways to improve dream recall. Getting a full night's sleep can sharpen recall. Since the longest dream period is usually at the end of our sleep period, people who have difficulty recalling their dreams should try not to wake up too suddenly. Instead, they should lie in a passive and relaxed state for a minute or two. Sometimes the first thought that comes into mind may bring back the dream. Later in the day some incident may remind the dreamer of the dream (Chetwynd, 1980).

Setting up a special time for telling dreams is a good way for children to remember them. It also encourages children to be more open and make it easier to discuss other private experiences or problems (Gackenbach & Bosveld, 1989). Many families use the breakfast hour as their special time to share their dreams.

Using autosuggestion before going to bed is another good way to remember dreams. As the children are going to sleep, ask them to try and remember their dreams in the morning. Using a pre-sleep suggestion can help such as, "You will remember your dreams when you wake up." The phrase should be repeated as the child is going to sleep.

Reliving the dream in reverse can help recall. We usually remember the end of the dream upon awakening more than the beginning. Instead of going back to the beginning, try reliving the dream from the end and working backwards to the beginning. Ask successively, "What happened before this? What brought me to this point?" And so, if one's child tells a dream fragment, it can be useful to respond, "Well, what was happening in the dream just before that?"

One of the best ways to keep from either simply forgetting about a dream or jumping to conclusions concerning its meaning is to start a dream journal. Taking the time to write down a dream usually helps the dreamer to remember it in greater detail. It also provides a permanent record to which to return. By recording a dream and what it appears to mean, we can check back later to see if we were correct in our understanding of its meaning (Milligan, 1997).

<u>Keeping A Dream Journal</u>

Recording dreams can be boring at times. Parents can help keep it interesting and fun for the child. Using a special book for the dream journal can make it more personalized for the child. Let the child choose the book herself from a variety of blank journals found in stationery stores. Have the child fill the book with pictures of clouds or other images that the child relates to sleeping and dreaming. After recording the dream, have the child draw pictures in the journal of one or more images from the dream.

When recording dreams, the date should be included along with the feelings that were experienced during and after the dream. Anything important that may have been going on in the waking life of the dreamer should also be included. A pen and paper should be kept next to the bed so that the dream can be recorded immediately. If the entire dream can not be remembered, just a key word or phrase can be recorded, usually this will bring back the dream. If no images or words can be remembered then just record the feelings the dream brought. Writing anything at all in the journal daily will help with improving the recall.

If the child is too young to take part in the writing of the journal, the parent needs to do it for her. Along with recording the dream, also record any events that may be related to the dream, such as an argument, being exhausted from a trip, something frightening that happened, medicine that was taken, or any non-routine events. These facts are especially important for understanding any nightmares or sleepwalking episodes (Garfield, 1984).

We usually dream in series. After the child has been recording dreams for a month or so, important ideas or themes may be seen running through them. There may be some problem that the child has been working on that the parent hasn't noticed before. This can lead to a conversation on what the child is dealing with in waking life.

Interviewing For Dream Content

It is important that a child should not be pressured to remember a dream. It's possible that if pushed too hard, the child will just make something up in order to please. A child should be reassured that it is okay not to remember a dream. Nor should a child be rewarded for remembering a dream and punished for not remembering. This could lead to confabulation or story telling (Foulkes, 1982).

Younger children don't always understand the concept of what a dream is. If this is the case, questions can be asked without using the word dream, such as: "What were you seeing" or "What was happening just before you woke up?" It is possible a child may confuse the question, "What were you dreaming?" with "Tell me a story." This is especially true for very young children. For example, when three-year-old Timmy was asked what he dreams about, he began to tell a long story about how he dreamed the police were putting people in jail. He was playing with small police cars at the time and thoroughly enjoying his game.

A dream may arise from something the child was doing shortly before bedtime or earlier in the day. Alternatively, it may symbolize the child's feelings towards an ongoing issue that he is wrestling with at a deeper level of his consciousness. Or it may evolve out of a memory that holds special meaning for him. Some dreams fall between positive developmental dreams and fantastical ones. Some dreams are purely entertaining. If you cannot discover how the child's dream is linked to his life, feelings, or activities, treat it as a creative springboard for the child. Do not struggle to find meaning where there may be none or it is too well hidden.

Dr. Pam Spurr (1999) suggests that when the child recounts a dream, you may want to try to determine both the type of dream he has experienced and the meaning behind images and events. You can ask him questions related to key areas, which may be summarized in the following DREAM key:

DETAIL: What details stand out in the child's recollections?
RECOGNITION: Did the child recognize people, places or feelings in his dream?
EMOTIONS: What was the overriding emotion experienced during the course of the dream?
ACTION: Did the child take an active or passive role in the dream?
MEANING: What does the child think the dream means?

For all ages, some topics to be explored are characters, settings, activities, the dreamer's own role in the dream, feelings, and the degree to which the dream content was visualized. Gayle Delaney (1989), in her book *Living Your Dreams*, suggests asking these questions:

- Describe the opening setting of the dream.
- Does it remind you of anything?
- Describe the characters in your dream.
- What is your relationship with the characters?
- What are the major objects in the dream?
- What do the objects remind you of?
- What are the major events or actions in the dream?
- What do these events or actions remind you of?
- What feelings were you having in the dream?
- What were you feeling when you woke up?
- Do you have any ideas on what this dream might mean?

There may be times when a child will remember a dream but is reluctant to talk about it. By using artwork, the child can express himself other than verbally. Crayons, markers, colored pencils and paint can be used to make a pictorial telling of the dream. Several sheets of blank paper can be made into a dream book. Along the way, or when finished, the child can explain the dream through the artwork (Scallion, 1987).

Dreams Make Us Aware Of Something Needed In Waking Life

Dreams can help us detect the unconscious aspects of our personalities. By identifying the traits of the people who appear in our dreams, we can catch sight of our unconscious attitudes, actions, and habits. Emotions and thoughts that may not necessarily express our true selves may be represented. We all have unconscious tendencies, of which we are completely unaware, operating within us.

A dream is often trying to call our attention to something needed in waking life, something that may have been ignored or forgotten. This is especially true with recurrent dreams. Once the message is apparent, the dreams usually stop. Frequently the characters and circumstances in the dream are interpreted as actually being related to those same people and conditions in waking life. In such cases, there is often a hidden message or lesson in the symbols and actions seen in the dream. However, the dream may be calling attention to a certain aspect of the dreamer's life. Perhaps the meaning of a dream is to look more closely at the relationship we have in waking life with the things we dream about (Thurston, 1978).

Sudden changes in dream patterns or content could signal a problem. A sudden increase in nightmares, insomnia, and anxiety can sometimes be the result of certain medications (See Appendix A). Changes in children's dreams can also be caused by a sleep disorder or by a major life change.

There is another reason why dreams may change; for adults and for some children, dreaming changes are sometimes associated with the onset of depression. If a person normally has a mixture of happy, sad, and frightening dreams and suddenly the dreams change to dark, gloomy, or with very few people in them, the dreamer may be developing a depressive illness (Hartmann, 1987). The opposite is true as well. If the dreams are suddenly becoming more lively and active with more people in them, this may indicate that a period of depression is lifting.

Dreams can be sensitive to subtle body changes of which the person is not aware. For example, a man dreams something is squeezing his heart and later suffers from a heart attack. Dreams such as these are rare, but if the dream is really traumatic and relates to a specific part of the body, it's at least worth checking out at the next medical visit.

When Should Dreams Be Considered Guidance?

One of the most challenging tasks in dreamwork is to evaluate the accuracy of dream "guidance." Sometimes the dream seems to say without a doubt that we should follow a particular pursuit - a new job, a trip or some type of activity. When should the dream be taken as a literal statement of something we should do?

Lacy had a dream that she had a Native American mandala tattooed on her head. The next day she went and had the back of her lower head shaved and had a mandala actually tattooed on her skull. In a later interview, she was asked if she had considered the possibility that the dream may have meant she should study Native American symbolism - to put it *in* her head not *on* her head. She admitted she had not thought of that. A better way would be to see the dream as one possibility, as one course of action that may be considered. How does it turn out in the dream?

Angels in dreams may symbolize guidance, wisdom, and the light of truth (Sechrist, 1968). The angel may be actually directing the dreamer in some way or leading the dreamer in some direction. The angel may represent that the dreamer is on the right path. Angel figures could also be a warning that the dreamer is going the wrong way (Chetwynd, 1980). The dreamer should note what the angel looks like and the action taking place. Did the dream feel good or was it scary? Although sometimes we misunderstand what's being presented in our dreams, and a fearful reaction is not indicative of that symbol being inherently threatening.

There comes a point where the guidance in the dream must be evaluated. You shouldn't just blindly follow the advice, as Lacy did. Thurston (1988) lists several criteria that can be used to evaluate the guidance:
- Does the guidance have the "ring of truth" to it?
- Does it fit with the *best* that I know I should be doing, not just something acceptable?

- Does it help me see things beyond my conscious understanding? Does it stretch me to see things in a new way?
- Does the guidance seem reasonable?
- In the dream, who is presenting the guidance? Is that the sort of person in waking life whom I trust?
- Does the guidance leave me feeling hopeful about my life?
- If I apply the guidance, can I expect to see benefits coming to me and to *all* others involved?
- Would following this guidance give me peace of mind?
- Does a trusted close friend agree with my interpretation?

For a child, the most fruitful way of recognizing guidance is to look at from whom the guidance is coming. For example, the child's parents are the people she would trust the most, so the guidance would probably be good. Unless it just feels wrong to the child, if she knows that it will do harm to someone. If the guidance is coming from someone she doesn't trust or from someone who is always doing the wrong thing, then the guidance should be evaluated more fully.

Exploring Emotion In Dreams

Emotions during dreams is very significant. Therefore, not analyzing feelings can limit the interpretation of the dream. If the dreamer has trouble identifying the feelings, then a step back might be in order, and a look at the dream as if it is a story. What is the character in the story feeling? For example, the dog was angry or the doll was sad. This is a way of looking at the dream objectively or as a passive observer (Milligan, 1997).

Your child may be able to tell you that he had a dream, but when questioned he can tell you nothing of what has actually happened in the dream. Often younger children experience feelings they cannot label, while children of all ages sometimes find it hard to describe and discuss problems with their parents. In their dreams, these feelings or problems may be experienced as emotion without accompanying images (Spurr, 1999).

If your child describes a feeling or 'sense' to you without being able to give you any details, discuss the feelings he recalls, and ask him if he is reminded of any feelings he has experienced during waking hours. This may give you clues as to what has caused the discomfort that has been transferred to the dream.

Five-year-old Emma was spending the weekend with her grandmother. She woke in the morning and said she had a bad dream. Emma's grandmother asked her if she could tell her about the dream, but the little girl couldn't recall any details. The grandmother then began to gently question Emma. Is there anything bothering you? Are you mad about something? Are you unhappy about something? Are you sad or afraid? Suddenly Emma cried out, "I miss my mommy!"

Children can't always identify the emotions they are feeling so will often act out in anger instead. Warren (1990) gives some definitions and causes of anger in adult and children:

- The capacity to become angry is an impressive gift, which comes as part of our biological inheritance.
- Anger is a physical state of readiness. When we are angry we are prepared to act.
- The whole purpose of anger is to give us the wherewithal for managing our environment - particularly those parts that cause us to feel hurt, frustrated, or fearful. If we do that poorly, we will regularly experience a sense of inadequacy and helplessness.

The most important factor in handling anger, continues Warren, is to get our self-concept into shape. The main reason for this is that when our self-concept is well put together, and we have a plentiful supply of self-esteem, we have ample energy to run our lives. Also, fewer things will make us angry. Like all of us, children become angry when they perceive a situation or person as frustrating, threatening, or hurtful. But, unlike adults, children do not have the power to make radical changes in their lives. They have a weak power base, little autonomy, and only occasional independence.

Unlike most adults, children do not have a self-system in place. They live with parents or other adults who are there to help them in the formation of a self-system and self-concept. Once children do possess a well-formed self-concept, usually they still lack the knowledge and experience to interpret the world in relation to themselves. The formation of children is within the care of their parents.

When adults express anger, they do it from a power base. When children express anger, they do it from a dependent state, as well as from their immature understandings. When adults are angry, they usually know what is wrong and what they wish would change. When children are angry, sometimes they know why, but often they don't.

Nine-year-old Rosie kept having dreams in which she was angry at her mother. She couldn't understand these dreams because in waking time they weren't having any problems. While talking with a counselor, it was discovered that Rosie was actually angry at her siblings. Rosie was the youngest of three children and had an older brother and sister. She felt as though they were constantly picking on her. Since they were older, Rosie felt powerless to stop the abuse or to retaliate. Rosie rarely confided in her mother about the situation because she didn't want to be a "tattletale."

According to Campbell (1999), the mother is often the target of a child's anger. The mother is the child's safe haven. In Rosie's case, she felt that her mother should have taken care of the conflict she was having with her siblings. Even though Rosie didn't "tell" on her siblings, she felt as though her mother should know and do something about it. In a child's eyes, mother should be able to fix everything.

Sometimes the emotion one is feeling in the dream will have a different effect upon awakening. Ten-year-old Tina's parents were going through a divorce. Tina had a dream in which there was a small fire in her house. Tina and her mother were in the front yard watching. Tina wanted to go inside and put out the fire but her mother said, "No, don't go in, everything is lost." Tina went in anyway with a hose and put out the fire. Tina awoke feeling happy and excited. She had "saved the day." However, sadly, Tina found out she had not saved the day, her parents were still getting divorced. Children often think that they can save their parents' marriage, and when they can't, they may feel that it's their fault.

Waking up feeling guilty about a dream may prevent a child from sharing it with a parent. Six-year-old Mikey had a dream that his mother had caught him stealing money out of her purse. The preceding day Mikey had been begging his mother to buy him a toy, but she refused. Mikey woke from the dream crying. Alarmed, his mother tried to find out what the dream was about, but Mikey felt too guilty and ashamed to tell her.

Dreams For Healing

Can dreams heal? Research has shown that there is a direct communication between our brain and our immune cells (Gackenbach & Bosveld, 1989). This communication shows up neurochemically and anatomically. There are nerve fibers between the brain and other parts of the body, providing a direct communication between the central nervous system and the immune cells.

Achterberg (1984) points to the central role of emotions as a starting point for an understanding of how imagery may affect immunity. Because both imagery and emotions are located in the same vicinity in the brain, they may share certain biochemical wiring. Many of the autonomic functions associated with health and disease are emotionally triggered. The same basic communication system that connects our emotional state to our autonomic systems may also exist for imagery.

Verbal messages, continues Achterberg, must undergo translation by the imagery system before they can be understood by the involuntary or autonomic nervous system. Although there's no need to examine these feelings while we are healthy, if we become ill, gaining access to and controlling our imaginal processes may be more important than we realize. Consciously accessing and manipulating images may prove to be a way to enter into psychophysiological systems and establish harmony in functions and structures that have gone awry.

Haskell (1985) states that whatever is dreamed is real in terms of physiological response. Researchers have found a connection between what people fantasize or imagine and the biological activity involved in actually performing those activities. For example, visualizing yourself doing a particular action, say lifting an object, the muscles in the arm you were thinking about show increased electrical activity. Studies show that subjects salivate more when asked to produce images of their favorite foods than when they thought of food they dislike. Imagining an object moving across the sky produces more oculomotor (eye) movements than visualizing a stationary object (Gackenbach & Bosveld, 1989).

Simonton, a radiation oncologist, experimented with imagery as therapy with his cancer patients. The process is described as a period of relaxation, during which the patient mentally pictures a desired goal or result. For the cancer patient, it would mean visualizing the cancer, the treatment destroying it, and the body's natural defenses helping the patient recover. The success with this imagery therapy was impressive as case after case, the patient's cancer went into remission after extensive work with imagery (Simonton, Matthews-Simonton, & Creighton, 1981).

According to Gackenbach & Bosveld (1989), clinical work with healing imagery has found four components to be crucial to the image's effectiveness:
1. The image should be vivid and resonant for the individual.
2. Being involved in the process of imaging is more important than the image itself.
3. The image should be spontaneous and chosen by the individual so that he is comfortable with it.
4. The imager/dreamer should feel in control of the process.

Anyone can try this type of imagery for healing. Before going to sleep clearly see in your mind's eye the condition that needs healing. Then visualize the desired outcome. Hold the images in your mind while falling asleep. For example, 12-year-old Bessie has asthma. She loves the outdoors and is involved in several different sports. However, she was being hindered by her respiratory problems. She began using imagery before going to sleep, imagining she was running, swimming and playing softball with no adverse effects. Soon her dreams started to reflect this improvement, containing themes of participating effortlessly in sporting events. Bessie was able to cut back on her asthma medication during waking life.

Some healing dreams come spontaneously. In *The Healing Power of Dreams*, Garfield (1991) writes about some examples of healing dreams. One such dream was from a woman who was suffering from arthritis. In her previous dreams, she often had images of her arms being in a straitjacket. Her dreaming mind had compared her limited mobility to the forced restriction of the jacket.

However, one night she dreamed that she slipped on ice, but was able to get up easily. She awoke to find her arthritic condition greatly improved. In her dream the woman was healed; the healing carried over into the waking state.

There are dream themes that can indicate that the dreamer is returning to health. These images, or signposts, are often of "new" things. For example, the dreamer sees green grass and lush fields; the dreamer sees blossoming trees; and the dreamer sees a newborn puppy. Other images may be metaphors of a new body image that is evolving as the dreamer heals. For example, the dreamer sees a new or restored house; the dreamer finds a lost watch; and the dreamer was wearing new clothes. Preventing a car accident or maneuvering down a hazardous road could depict the dreamer's returning sense of control over life (Garfield, 1991).

Re-dreaming The Dream

Re-dreaming the dream is a technique that can be used to select a more positive response to the dream events. It involves using the imagination in the waking state to re-dream the events up to the point at which the dreamer's response is not an ideal one. At that point in the re-dreaming experience, using a reverie fashion, the dreamer can change his own response to the action taking place in the dream (Thurston, 1978).

Re-dreaming can also be used to create a new ending to the dream. Upon awakening (or at a later time), the dreamer can use his imagination to continue the dream onward. It can either be written out or just fantasized. The dream can then be taken in a new direction or have a different and more resolved ending (Siegel, 1996). Imagination can also be used to prepare for better dreams by picturing a dream scenario while falling asleep. The ending can be whatever the dreamer wants it to be.

Another option is to go back to sleep to re-dream the dream. In this way you can reenter the dream and change the ending. Kaplan (1999) gives an example of this technique: A woman dreamed she was in a room with two men. They started to attack her. One man held her down while the other man approached holding a needle in a threatening position. She awoke terrified, but before any damage could be done. She decided to re-dream the dream. Immediately returning to sleep, the woman was able to reenter the dream. In her new version, she was able to use martial arts to kick the men away from her and then flee to safety. [See section on Nightmare Help for a more detailed description of the re-dreaming method with children.]

Reentering/Revisiting A Good Dream

Sometimes we want to hold on to our good dreams a while longer. Good dreams are nice to come back to after a rough day, just to have fun with, or as a way to help us relax as we go to sleep. This technique is easy for children. The child may have a favorite dream that can be used or a fantasy can be envisioned. For example, five-year-old Hanna had a magical dream in which she was a lovely princess, climbing huge castle steps. Dr. Pam Spurr (1999) describes the process, using the power of suggestion:

- At bedtime suggest to the child that she should recount the main parts of the dream/fantasy and how it makes her feel.
- Ask the child if she'd like to revisit it. Tell her to close her eyes and picture the vivid images that she remembers.
- As she settles down quietly suggest a story line, such as in Hanna's case: "Hanna, I can see you as a beautiful princess, in the sunshine, climbing up and up to your very own beautiful castle ..."

Using Lucid Dreaming Therapeutically

Many people have found that they can use lucid dreams to deal with troubling conflicts in their lives. Some dreamers have applied lucidity to overcoming phobias. For example, a man who was very fearful of heights used his lucid dreams of flying to gradually rise higher and higher. As he became able to ascend further in his dreams without discomfort, his waking apprehension gradually decreased (Van de Castle, 1994).

There are two main ways that lucid dreaming is initiated. The first type is "wake initiated," which begins during brief periods of arousal and then continue on as the dreamer returns to sleeping REM. Usually, the dreamer experiencing this type of lucidity will be aware both of having been momentarily awake and of having gone back to sleep. The majority of lucid dreams, however, begin with an ordinary dream. Known as "dream-initiated" lucid dreams, they usually occur after something causes the dreamer to suddenly become aware that he is dreaming. It's the "oh, this is a dream" sense, attested to by almost all lucid dreamers (LaBerge & Rheingold, 1990).

There are a few signs that can indicate to a dreamer that he has turned lucid. One major dream sign is phenomena that can't occur in waking life, such as walking through walls. Objects with writing on them is another sign. Every time you look at it, the writing will be different. Frequent lucid dreamers will have their own personal dream signs.

One way to induce lucid dreams is by using autosuggestion (See section on Nightmare Help for more techniques). After you've been recording your dreams for awhile you will be able to see that certain objects or symbols reappear from time to time. You can choose one of these symbols as a focal point for inducing lucidity. For example, if your dreams frequently contain a black cat, you can say to yourself during the day or before you fall asleep at night that the next time you see the black cat you will recognize that you are dreaming. This may be able to trigger lucidity. Another type of autosuggestion is to tell yourself before falling asleep that you want to have a particular theme or that you want to have a lucid dream (Gackenbach & Bosveld, 1989).

Knowing the reasons behind a dream can eliminate needless worry, particularly if the dream has
recurred.

—Gillian Holloway, Ph.D. in *The Complete Dream
Book: Discover What your Dreams Tell about You
and Your Life*

Chapter 8
Why We Should Pursue Bad Dreams

Paying attention to our troubling dreams can improve our chances of reducing stress and anxiety in our waking lives. Dreams tell us things that we need to know to function more effectively when we're not dreaming. They inform us about conditions that require corrective action and often give hints as to which plans might be successful. Studies done by Van de Castle (1994) show that negative or unpleasant dreams are remembered more frequently than positive dreams.

A fear of nightmares or other anxieties about dreams can block dream recall. This can usually be overcome by learning about the dreams and by recognizing that the majority of nightmares represent opportunities for personal healing through emotional release. Dreams that evoke emotion frighten us (Kaplan, 1999). They are often indirectly warning us about psychological imbalances or current behavior patterns that need to be remedied if we don't want the unpleasant dreams to continue.

Discovering What Is Going On In Waking Life

Examining children's dreams is a good way of becoming aware of any inner conflict they may be experiencing that the parent may not know. A nightmare or frightening dream may be useful in uncovering these struggles (Hartmann, 1987). A frightening dream can sometimes provide a view of how the dreamer's mental state is changing. We've seen earlier how a dream can predict or reflect an illness. If nightmares aren't addressed, they could lead to problems in waking life such as sickness, accidents or relationship conflicts.

We should work with all of our dreams and the personal issues they raise. If an image is disturbing, try to find out why. If a dream frightens you, talk about it with someone (Gackenbach & Bosveld, 1989). A nightmare forces the dreamer to recognize that there is conflict in waking life. If we continuously ignore our frightening dreams we may begin to suffer emotionally.

Buried feelings, like truth, sooner or later, will find their way out. Eventually these concerns demand acknowledgement or resolution and solace. For many, this unfinished business surfaces in our dreams. Unfinished business keeps us stuck, keeps things from getting comfortably stored or filed away, which is why recurring dreams are so common. Surely, it is better that we find a way to use dreams for our own good rather than leaving them unattended (Wiseman, 1989).

The silver lining of painful nightmares is that through the often transparent symbolism, they shine a spotlight on the issues that are the most upsetting, yet un-expressible for the child. Every nightmare, no matter how distressing, contains vital information about crucial emotional challenges in the child's life. To a parent whose ears and heart is open, listening to the most distressing nightmares is like hearing the child's unconscious, speaking directly, delivering a special call for help (Siegel & Bulkeley, 1998).

Self-Esteem

Many people, including children, blame themselves whenever something goes wrong. They turn their anger inward. By turning the anger inside, they don't feel the anger, instead they feel hurt. Blaming themselves for every problem often then turns to guilt. Often negative messages are sent to them in their dreams. There may be feelings of despair, depression and feelings of helplessness and hopelessness. Because depression is a major source of anger, a destructive cycle can result from this type of self-abuse. People who turn their anger inward usually feel as though they have lost control over some situation in their life (Campbell, 1999).

A young girl who was having nightmares would pray to Jesus every night, pleading not to have any more bad dreams. When her prayers weren't answered and the nightmares continued the girl thought the dreams occurred because she was a bad girl. The girl thought that bad dreams meant bad person (Avila, 1999). This way of thinking will surely lead to guilt. Guilt will often lead to self-esteem issues. What's wrong with me? Why am I so bad? Guilt intensified can lead to other things such as emotional and behavior problems.

There could be many reasons why people turn their anger inward. It could be genetic or their personality type. It is common to inadvertently train our children to handle anger in this way. If the parent criticizes and blames the children, the children in turn may respond by blaming and criticizing themselves. They may also then develop the habit of turning their anger inward. Other children may mimic the parent by criticizing and blaming someone else. These children may develop habits of refusing to take responsibility for their own behavior and of blaming others. Both of these means of handling anger are destructive (Campbell, 1999).

Displaced Anger

A primary lifetime conflict for a person is his own anger. It is essential that parents teach their children how to handle anger effectively. Displaced anger often uses innocent people as targets. This most often occurs when the person is angry with someone they can not confront, such as parents or teachers. Sometimes parents will vent their anger on their children. Children cannot tolerate parental anger, because they have no defenses against it (Campbell, 1999).

This can sometimes be seen in children's dreams when the character turns into a monster or a villain. Garfield (1984) explains that children will often veil fear-producing adults in their lives. Adults who lose their temper during the day or are cruel to each other, to a sibling, or to the child directly creep into the children's dreams at night in disguise. Sometimes they pull on the skin of beasts. Often they dress up as villains, ghosts, or monsters.

The demons of children's dreams are often - although not always - those people they love the most or depend on the most. Mother, father, sister, brother, significant relative, friend, even parts of the self, don mask and costume and chase children down the corridors of their dreams. For a young child to become aware that the villains of one's nightmares are frequently those people close to him is almost unbearable. Rather than seeing a parent as a wicked person, the parent is often depicted in the child's dream as a wicked dream character.

For example, seven-year-old Lenore had a dream in which her mother turned into a vampire. In waking life the girl's parents had been divorced. The mother had remarried and had another child by her second husband. This marriage was also rocky. The mother often used Lenore as a confidante for all of her complaints. Lenore was angry and felt as though her mother was draining her of energy, hence the vampire image (Garfield, 1984).

Another common dream theme for a child's displaced anger is monsters. Children have different kinds of monsters in their dreams, and the action involved varies. For example, if the parents are fighting a lot, the child may dream of shouting monsters. When a monster is hiding in the closet or under the bed, this makes the situation doubly scary, because there is nowhere safe or off-limits. According to Holloway (2001), creatures in the room or icky things like bugs in the bed tend to represent situations, while monsters tend to represent specific people. Therefore, when a monster is chasing the child in a dream, or yelling and threatening, this is a clue that the monster may represent a person in the child's life. Children's dream monsters not only reflect the tension, fear, and anger they feel during a conflict, but they dramatically show how frightening it is when the people they trust behave strangely.

Parents need to know that when they yell or exhibit unexpectedly harsh behavior either toward their children or towards others, this sometimes translates into monster dreams. A cranky teacher or scary neighbor can also be the human side of the monster. These dreams are not necessarily a signal of abuse or anything horrific, but they do indicate that the child may be experiencing something stressful, usually regarding someone close to her.

One more common theme for this issue is when something ordinary and perfectly harmless turns threatening. Although this may not always be about anger it could reflect tension in the child about some situation in waking life. Holloway (2001) gives the following example:

The boy dreamed often of being chased by a maniacal ball of yarn. He would be chased around in circles, and the faster he ran, the more the yarn gained on him. In his case, the dream seemed to reflect a tension between his mother (a knitter) and himself. He tried to please her by being as perfect as possible, but the more he strove for an unreachable goal the more pressured he felt (p. 42).

The theme of something ordinary, even beloved (such as a favorite toy), turning into a threat suggests that the child may be struggling with some situation or person that is usually known and kind, but may sometimes seem inexplicably difficult and harsh. The real-life parallel to the dream may be that the child is dealing with something that seems fine most of the time, but occasionally seems to turn against him. This could be anything from a playground buddy who occasionally plays unfairly to a situation at home that becomes confusing because it flips back and forth between normal and unsettling.

It is important that parents take the time to talk with their children about any difficulties they might be having. Talking about unpleasant dreams is a good beginning. As parents talk they should be able to see how the child responds to problems. Parents can teach their children to respond to difficulties in optimistic ways.

If you suspect you may be reflected in these monster sagas, then be understanding with the child and encourage him to share these dreams with you. You can use such reports to inform you when things have been unsettling to your child, and you can try to provide extra support and confidence during this phase. In some cases, of course, the monster may reflect someone other than a parent in your child's life. This is more common among school-age children who must contend with the expectations of peers and teachers. Encourage the child to share his nightmares with you, but do not interrogate him about what they might mean. Choose another time to ask whether there are kids at school, teachers, or neighbors that he finds scary.

Chapter 9
Nightmare Help

You should never dismiss a child's nightmare by saying something such as, "It's just a dream, it doesn't mean anything, just forget it." That won't help the child; it discounts his anxiety. A nightmare should at least be acknowledged. Parents should let the child know that his feelings and fantasies matter. Disregarding a nightmare could make the child afraid to go to sleep, afraid he'll have another nightmare. There are numerous different ways to work with and control dreams and nightmares. This is possible because nightmares usually occur in the lighter stages of sleep, which makes dreams easier to control (Pearce, 1999).

However, there is a debate about whether or not the content of a dream should actually be controlled. The focus in dream control should be on learning how to control one's response to dream events, not on controlling the creation of those events (Gackenbach & Bosveld, 1989). For example, the dreamer can confront and work with a scary dream image instead of just destroying it or running away.

The terror that lingers after a nightmare may accentuate a child's insecurity and bring on anxiety for hours or even days afterward. It may even disturb his ability to sleep by inducing insomnia, or fears and phobias about sleeping and dreaming. The parent can help the child restore his capacity to sleep and to harness the healing and creative potential of scary dreams by helping him break the spell of his nightmares (Siegel & Bulkeley, 1998). Even very young children can learn to encounter and overcome the threatening creatures of their nightmares. While there are numerous techniques that can be used to work with nightmares the following methods are especially good for children. These methods can be used before, during or after experiencing a nightmare.

Dreamercises

Dr. Pam Spurr (1999) has devised simple, creative techniques she calls Dreamercises to enable parents to help their children enjoy dreaming and to derive the most benefit from their dreams. Using dreamercises also tends to increase self-confidence as children develop their creativity and problem-solving skills. There are several dreamercises that can be useful for nightmares.

Control Panel Dreamercise

The Control Panel dreamercise gives the child the opportunity to talk about something that is bothering him and enables him to take control of a nightmare, so that he will no longer be frightened of dreaming. It can also be used purely as a creative drawing and dream-enhancing exercise. This dreamercise can be adapted to suit a child of any age, whatever his needs. Choose a quiet time when the child seems happy to open up a little, you do not necessarily have to wait until bedtime.

- Explore the child's nightmare in order to discover whatever may be troubling him.
- Give the child a large sheet of drawing paper and ask him to draw a control panel on it. Encourage him to use his imagination. The control panel can resemble that of any vehicle, from a spaceship to a car.
- Ask the child to fill in masses of detail and to tailor it to suit his specific needs. For example, the child may want to include on his panel a dump button to "dump" unwanted nightmares, or an eject button to "eject" any frightening thoughts. This is the opportunity for him to draw what will be most helpful to him.
- Let the child take pride in his finished control panel. Pin it above his bed so he can see it easily when he needs a boost to his confidence.
- At bedtime talk to the child about his control panel. Remind him that he is now master of his dreams.

Bash The Baddy Dreamercise

The Bash the Baddy dreamercise is perfect when the parent feels that strong action is needed to prevent the recurrence of a nightmare in the child. It is designed to increase the child's confidence after a frightening experience and to reassure him that the parent is on his side. After establishing the root cause of the nightmare, try any of the techniques described below to help the child obliterate the nightmare images and overcome the problem.

- When the child is feeling secure and communicative, either during the day or at bedtime, try the Bash the Baddy dreamercise.
- Ask the child to draw the nightmare image or to visualize it. Try to incorporate as much action as possible.
- Next you could ask the child to draw himself as a very large giant and the nightmare image as tiny in comparison. He can then visualize what he, as a

giant, would do to the tiny nightmare image. Alternatively, he could tear up the picture of his nightmare image while repeating an affirmative statement such as: "Now you can't frighten me, you're going in the garbage!" If the child is quite young he can hand the picture to his parent and say, "My parent is going to take care of you! Good Bye!"

- Tell the child confidently that he has the power to change frightening images into non-threatening ones. Advise him to "bash the baddy" right out of his dream if the nightmare returns.

Superhero Dreamercise

The Superhero dreamercise is designed primarily to prevent the recurrence of nightmares. Unlike the Bash the Baddy dreamercise, where nightmare images are disposed of in creative ways, the Superhero dreamercise allows the child to escape from involvement with the feared image by becoming a superhero.

- Ask the child, if he could be any superhero what talents would he choose to have. Would he be able to fly? Or perhaps he could disappear simply by saying some magic words. Let the child be as creative as he wants to be.
- Make a list of the talents of the child's superhero. Then star the most important talent on the list.
- For younger children, suggest they draw a picture of themselves as the superhero. They can have fun with details. For example they can draw a mask or a cape.
- Ask the child to imagine that he is the superhero. Tell him that if his nightmare comes back, he can put his special superhero talents into operation. For example, if his star talent is to be able to disappear, he could use this ability, if the nightmare recurred, to avoid seeing the nightmare image. Encourage him to use more than one of his superhero talents. For example, once he has disappeared, he might be able to fly away to his favorite place.
- Reassure him that he can do these things in his dreams.

Paper-Stage Approach

Anne Wiseman (1989) developed a method for solving dream problems, which she calls auto-drama. Initially developed for working with large groups of dreamers, Wiseman borrowed from Gestalt psychology, psychosynthesis, and psychodrama, creating the mini-system for working with dreams. Wiseman calls this process "mapping a problem on the paper-stage." The paper-stage approach is the method of putting the dream on paper. The dreamer tells the story of the dream with visual images instead of auditory images. The dream can then be worked on either by the dreamer alone or with the help of a guide.

As the dream story is laid out on paper, it can be understood visually to all observers. The dream details are turned into colored paper symbols, which then can be invested with the proper characteristics, attitudes, and emotions. Color, size, and shape play an important part. Color is a language in itself, giving the guide, as well as the dreamer, a great deal of information. What could take weeks to explain verbally are immediately visible with this method.

We usually wake from nightmares the moment we feel totally victimized, on the verge of being caught or killed. We jump out of our skins. It is as though the dream maker has sacrificed the dreamer's life, and this is, perhaps, the definition of a nightmare. Many children try to escape a bad dream by hiding under the covers or under the bed. As the guide, you can help stimulate more challenging and interesting possibilities than allowing the dream self to be sacrificed.

The Process

The next time your child is awakened by a bad dream, give support and comfort as usual, and when some measure of calm has been restored try acknowledging the monster (or other nightmare image). Tell the child to ask the monster not to come any more that night because everyone needs sleep. Say you'll talk about it in the morning - you'll even invite the monster to draw itself to prove how scary it is. Together you will look at it and find out more about this kind of fear.

The image language of dreams is richer and more colorful than the spoken language, more exquisitely concise and explicit than words. All we have to do is learn how to translate this picture back into feelings. That's why children are asked to draw their dreams and let the picture speak. When you harvest the feelings from the images, you have a life position statement in picture form. You almost always have an issue, a predicament or problem waiting to be acknowledged or solved.

Drawing the dream puts the dreamer in charge, so you start by giving the child some paper and felt markers or crayons. Wiseman likes to give them black felt markers for the drawing so that they can be photocopied. That way the monsters are firmly implanted on the paper and can't fade away. This helps to get the terror out of the head and down on paper where it can't move. On paper, the monster can't get you. Once the drawing is complete, there are several methods that can be used for working with the dream.

Reentering the Dream

After the dream has been captured on paper, the next step is to ask if the child feels safe enough to reenter the dream. The child needs to reenter the dream in order to confront the enemy and negotiate with it. The child may ask herself some questions, such as:
• How do I feel when I look at this dream picture?

- How can I make myself feel safe enough to reenter this scary dream?
- If I use my imagination, can I create a solution that saves my life?
- Is there a solution?
- If I feel helpless, who can help me? Who can I talk to?
- If no help is available, how can I help myself?
- If this dream would upset my parents, can I create a guide to help me?
- Is it fair for a dream monster to kill me?
- If I have the right to save my life, can I do it in every nightmare? (That's the challenge.)
- What are my strengths? When I feel bad about myself it helps to name them.
- What is the message in this dream? What is the gift in this dream?

If the dream is too scary, the child can draw in helpers or alternatives that shift the victim into a power position. If the child does not feel safe enough to reenter the dream, help the child create protection: a shield, a cage, or a telephone may help. Once the child is ready you can start with some questions, such as:
- How do you feel about drawing this scary nightmare?
- How will you make yourself feel safe enough to look at this monster again?
- If it is too scary, would it help to draw yourself outside of the picture?
- Close your eyes and let the monster draw itself.
- Create some helpers to give you courage. Draw them in.

Children are quick to think of ways to empower and protect the stuck self, such as:
- Drawing a shield.
- Becoming invisible.
- Capturing the monster in a cage or trap.
- Cutting the monster down to size.
- Getting help from an expert, a specialist, or a guide.
- Getting a ladder or parachute.
- Creating an army of friends.

Dialoguing With the Monster

Have the child consider the thought that the enemy may have something to tell the child about herself and her life. Don't kill it; instead dialogue with it. Consider its point of view. Maybe it has something to teach. The child can find out what power the monster has over her, and what the power is doing for her. The child can ask the monster what it wants and why it came. By talking and listening to its complaints, the child can better understand its anger and rage. Try whatever will enable the child to talk to the monster.

After the images in the drawing have been given a chance to speak, and after the child has heard all points of view, it is clearer what needs to happen to create a solution. The situation in the drawing can begin to move. Since all these voices are in some way a part of the dreamer, a settlement must be found that is fair to all of the internal participants. It is a challenge to find a way to live in peace with all the conflicting parts of oneself.

The child is given the chance to face a problem. And by listening and saying the dialogue, the child can actually exercise role reversal, explore new behavior, develop new understanding, and practice the art of negotiation. A behavior rehearsal is as good as experience. It moves the feelings. That alone empowers and creates an awareness that is the beginning of change.

When the child communicates with the monster, the monster almost always becomes more human. By the time it is invited to say what it wants and why it feels like attacking, the dreamer may begin to recognize her own buried angers or complaints. The monster's anger is often a mirror of the dreamer's own rage, frustration, or fear, of the unacceptable emotions that may have been repressed. Some questions the child may ask the monster include:

- Why have you come to scare me?
- What do you want?
- If I dare to stop running away, can we talk?
- If monsters represent giant feelings, what feelings do you represent?
- If you could talk, what would you say?
- How would you feel if I scared you like this?
- What's good about you?
- I'll tell you what's good about me.
- If we negotiate a deal, will you stop scaring me?

Recreating the Dream

Recreating the dream on paper allows the dreamer to experience it again, this time free of terror, and in a calmer frame of mind. Changing just one thing is usually enough to get the child moving towards a self-empowering solution. For example, the dreamer can give herself a stick or a shield in order to defend herself against the monster. It's possible to alter time, making it possible to go back and forth in different time frames. For example, the dream can be started over to change the actions.

Helpers vs Superpowers

The child may want to call upon real or imaginary helpers that aid in finding the way to a solution. Wiseman encourages reality and prefers specialists as helpers such as lawyers, guides, counselors, judges, or firemen, etc. She explains that employing superpowers may help for awhile, but in the end they are less satisfying than a self-empowering solution. Help can come from someone close such as a favorite teacher or relative. Let the child supply the dialogue; they know what they need better than anyone else.

Killing the Monster

Killing the monster may be the child's first instinct. Boys particularly love to spear and bloody the monster. It is safe enough to vent that power on paper, but the idea that the monster may return the next night twice as terrible helps them reconsider alternatives to killing. Since monsters very often reflect negative parts of ourselves, if we kill them, we kill that part of ourselves. We will never get the dream's message if we kill, nor will we understand why the dream sent this kind of messenger. If we are to learn to live with our own inner violence, anger, and hurt feelings, let us start by befriending our monsters. Find out why they have so much power over us. Our enemies always have the most to tell us about ourselves. It also helps to consider the idea that the monster may offer a gift by coming into our dream.

Finding Solutions

Because a lot of us have had little success coping with our own nightmares, we often feel helpless when we try to help our children. We all fear not knowing what to do. Most teachers and parents prefer to avoid not knowing.

This approach to creative resolutions requires dreamers to help themselves and to take responsibility for what they know. It establishes that only they know the usable answers, the proper steps on the path to change and the solutions to their own problems or protection for their limitations. Nightmare fears are calmed by the very act of seeking a solution equal to the nightmare. The effort alone threatens and weakens the oppressor and energizes the helpless. Children will recognize solutions that suit their readiness and their skills of the moment, and they will reject those that don't. Sometimes we must try a number of solutions before finding the one that works.

Fears. Fear is a reaction to danger or anticipated danger, and it is part of the body's normal defense mechanism. The physiological reactions associated with fear are rapid heart beat, loss of breath, paralysis, or muscle tension as the body prepares for flight or fight, or finds itself unable to move. When a child has a nightmare, it will take a little time just for the body to resume its normal functioning. Patience and comforting are the best help.

Fear is partly instinctive, but it is largely a learned response. Fear tells the body it needs to protect itself from real, anticipated, or imaginary danger. It tells us something bad is happening, could happen, or is about to happen, and that we should try to avoid it, or warn somebody, or stop. It tells us something is potentially wrong or too frightening to bear.

Fear usually tells us that more information is necessary before we can act in an emergency situation or cope with a challenge. If we have more information, we can usually deal with fear better, particularly if the fear surrounds something new we are supposed to do or try. It is a good rule to respect and honor fear. Fear generally can be considered an effective guide.

<u>Daring to draw.</u> Sometimes children are so frightened by their nightmares that they cannot even dare to draw them. If a dream has that kind of impact, the only way to dislodge it from the mind is to talk about it. There are numerous picture books about nightmares that children can read (see Appendix B), and it may help to look at children's pictures in books on nightmare help. Other children's solutions to nightmares may give the child courage and the knowing that other people experience nightmares.

<u>Being the guide.</u> If you are going to play the part of the guide, start with the assumption that you know nothing. Do not diminish fear. Do not give answers or solutions. Instead, ask for the dreamer to find her own answers; try several, see which option feels right. Help her find a solution that she can handle. You are simply a follower who asks very simple questions. You can commiserate, suggest new angles, and accompany the dream worker, but do not create the solution. Don't presume to understand the problem. Help the child find her own satisfaction.

Children are literal and that is the best approach to take with them and their dreams. Avoid the hidden meanings unless <u>they</u> recognize and make the connection, don't dwell on them. Remember that <u>you</u>, the adult authority, are very likely part of the problem. By working with the child you can help her with authority issues, and she can help you modify your power over her. As the guide, there are some useful questions that you can ask the child as she works on her dream:
- What will you do to help yourself in the picture?
- What could you suggest if you weren't so frightened?
- How will you make it less scary?
- Close your eyes and see yourself getting help. What do you see?
- If it could speak, what would it say?
- How can you control the monster so you can talk to it?
- Ask what it wants from you.
- What is his, her, or its point of view? Do you think it has a point?
- Then what?... Then what?... Then what?
- If you can't control or tame something, where can you put it?
- What would you like to tell the monster?
- If you had some power, what would you suggest?
- If there was a fair solution, what would it be?
- What would help?

- Call upon a specialist who knows about these things.
- See yourself getting help.
- See yourself finding a solution.

Tool Kit for Guides

1. The key to arriving at a solution is to respect the sequential progression, the child's concept of what comes next.
2. Think of it like a game of pick-up sticks. Without disturbing the pile, what stick can you dislodge next?
3. Consider that the child knows better than you what to do next.
4. The guide, with patience, willingly follows the child's sequential steps towards the solution, respecting obstacles.
5. Don't mistake detours and obstacles as resistance; simply assume you may be asking the wrong question or going in the wrong direction.
6. It is important to let the child take the lead because your assumptions, if not wrong, will probably be off the mark.
7. Careful use of the dreamer's own language helps to keep your assumptions from interfering with the dreamer's progress.
8. A solution may pose more fear than the problem itself. Don't forget to check that out first. For example, the fears of older children can be quite complex and sophisticated, therefore, more difficult to express and more difficult to determine. They may even be impossible to solve. What solution is there for children whose parents abuse them or whose parents are involved in a bitter divorce?
9. Joining the dreamer wherever the imagery takes you - *i.e.*, that is, communicating back to the child whatever images are coming up for you, the guide - establishes reverence and trust for the dreamer's authority and leadership. Only then can the dreamer afford to reveal the goals, the path to change, and the obstacles that block it.
10. Guiding simply helps the dreamer acknowledge what she already knows, but doesn't realize that she knows.
11. Nightmares are very likely to stir up strong emotions in the child, and it is important for the guide to acknowledge these feelings. Just as a wound must be cleansed before it can heal, anger, hatred, grief, and frustration need expression before forgiveness and spiritual healing can occur.
12. Work with the literal level of the dream, simply using the imagery provided by the dream without disturbing the hidden roots under the symbolic analogies. These roots are often too complicated and personal to look at directly, which may be why they come in disguise in the first place.
13. Respect the facts and don't argue with the reasons.

<u>When the Parent is Part of the Problem</u>. A certain amount of strain is built into every parent-child relationship. Some parents create undo stress in their children's lives, usually without intending to and without realizing it. Consider that you, the parent, may be a part of the child's problem, so that it may be difficult for the child to work through a dream with you. Don't press it. Let it go. Give them encouragement to work it through alone or with someone else. Children are often so locked into fidelity, they cannot betray their negative feelings about their parents for fear of rejection.

<u>Examples of the Paper-Stage Approach</u>.

Here are two examples from *Nightmare Help*, by Anne Wiseman (1989):

Joe (age 12) and "The Green Dinosaur Monster"

"I dreamed this giant dinosaur monster chased me all the way home. I ran and ran and just made it inside my house. I told my mother to look and see for herself. She said, 'You're just imagining it.' I looked out the window, and it was gone. That made me feel like a liar. If my mother can't see something, she won't believe me" (p. 40).

Joe's solution was worded this way: "I closed my eyes and let the picture speak to me. To make myself safe, I spoke to the dinosaur through the keyhole. I told him I don't like being chased. I just made it into my house. I had to make the door extra strong. With my eyes closed, I could hear him better. I asked the dinosaur what he was doing in my dream. He said, 'I'm scaring you.' I told him my mom won't believe me. She says you're only in my imagination. I tell him no one can see him but me, and to me he is real. He says, 'The things you imagine are the scariest things.' Now that I found the courage to talk to him, he's not so scary. Now I can see him, he is sort of real to me, like a new friend."

Joe faces three dilemmas in his dream - a monster that's chasing him, a parent who won't believe him, and a lively imagination full of fears. In his solution, the monster tells him the truth. Imaginary things are the scariest ones and saying they are not real doesn't help. When he and the monster agree, they become friends, and Joe's monster becomes an ally.

Here are some of the kinds of questions that might be good discussion starters with Joe:
- Do you have fears that adults pooh-pooh?
- How does it feel when you can't explain why you're afraid?
- What do you do when grown-ups don't believe you?
- How do you deal with feelings that big and dangerous?

Tim (age 11) and "The Screaming Robot"

"I dreamed that a monster robot was chasing me all over the house with alarm signals screaming and lights flashing. I was so scared I started to scream. My own noise woke me up. I didn't dare go back to sleep" (p. 38).

Tim's solution was worded this way: "I drew my dream and the way I made myself safe was to draw a turn-off switch on the robot so I could get it to stop flashing. Without juice, it couldn't even move. Then I closed my eyes to step back into the dream. Then I asked, 'What are you doing in my dream?' And the robot said, 'I just want you to play ball.' I said, 'If you want me to play ball, stop yelling and chasing me. You scare me when you chase me. I wish you were a little more human,' and that gave me the idea to draw him a heart. Once I got it to stop yelling, we could talk. When it talked about being a robot and all the hard work it does, I felt sorry and offered to help out on condition that I could play without getting scolded. My dad's inside that robot I think. I gave him a new heart. I hope it works."

Tim learned that if he could stand his ground, he could negotiate a way for the robot and the chased boy to get some of what they both needed. He recognized the voice, and gave it a heart. When it sounded more reasonable, he agreed to "play ball" if the robot would agree to stop shouting and flashing.

Here are some of the kinds of questions that might be good discussion starters with Tim:
- How is Dad like a robot?
- What does it mean to be like a robot?
- What does he mean "to play ball"?
- If a robot gets a heart, is it still a robot?

Lucid Dreaming

Lucid dreaming is being aware in the dream, knowing that you are dreaming. In a lucid dream the dreamer is able to control events somewhat. By being lucid in a nightmare, the dreamer can do many things, such as banish evil, confront a threatening character or just fly away. Alan Worsley, a British lucid dreamer, taught himself to wake up during frightening dreams. He could wake himself by shouting "Mother!" by the time he was five years old (Van de Castle, 1994).

By adding or removing images, the lucid dreamer has the ability to change her dreamscape, she can set things in motion, interact with whomever and whatever she wants, and determine the outcome of the dream. Being lucid during a nightmare, the dreamer can also call in a dream-friend to help confront an aggressive dream image. The dream-friend can be anyone that the child wants - a super-hero, a movie actor, or a parent. Taking charge of your dream life can help you take charge of your waking life as well.

Sarah was having recurring nightmares about being surrounded by hundreds of snakes. After learning how to become lucid while dreaming, she started zapping the snakes with a laser gun. The fear she felt in the dreams turned to a feeling of power and the nightmares stopped. Mary was having a dream in which she was driving her car when it suddenly hurtled over a cliff. As she was fearfully suspended in the air, she remembered that she could fly if she wanted to, and that's exactly what she did, coming to a safe landing on the ground. By coming up with these dream solutions, both Sarah and Mary became more self-confident and were able to take more charge in their waking lives.

Lucidity seems to create an environment in which the dream ego is less afraid of threatening dream figures or situations and is more willing to confront them. Paul Tholey (1988) offers some advice to lucid dreamers who find themselves face-to-face with a fearful dream figure:

1. Do not attempt to flee from a threatening dream figure. Rather, confront him courageously. Look at him openly and ask him in a friendly way, "Who are you?"
2. If it is possible to address the dream figure, try to come to a reconciliation with him through a constructive dialogue. If agreement is impossible, try to frame the conflict as an open dispute. Refuse his insults or threats, but recognize his justified objections.
3. Do not surrender to an attack by a dream figure. Show your readiness to defend yourself by taking a defensive position and by staring the dream figure in the eyes. If a fight is unavoidable, attempt to conquer the dream enemy, but do not try to kill. Offer reconciliation to the conquered enemy.
4. Attempt to reconcile with the hostile dream figure in thought, words, and/or gestures.
5. If a reconciliation does not seem possible, separate yourself from the figure in thought, word, and/or bodily withdrawal.
6. After reconciliation, ask the dream figure if he can help you. Then mention specific problems in your waking life with which you need help.

Lucid Dreaming Shouldn't Always Be Used

Using dream control may not always be good during a nightmare. In studies done by Gackenbach & Bosveld (1989), it was shown that in nightmare induced lucid dreams, control alleviated the negative emotions of the dreams only if the dreams were not remembered very well afterwards. If the dreamers had strong waking memories, however, negative emotions were also high regardless of the amount of dream control. This suggests that when one is lucid as a result of a fearful dream situation and further has access to waking memory, it may be preferable to go with the dream as it unravels, rather than try to direct the content. If, however, one is lucid and does not recall much of waking life, then directing the flow may be adaptive.

A second reason not to use lucid dreaming is that some lucid dreamers get in the habit of turning their nightmares into sweet dreams. The consciousness in their dreams may begin to function as it does in waking life, complete with its unconscious defenses, such as denial or avoidance. The very appearance of dream consciousness contaminates the dream with the attitudes and the way in which the dreamer copes in waking life. It is often better for a person to wake up from a horrible nightmare than from a sugarcoated lucid dream. The nightmare forces the dreamer to recognize, however superficially, that he is conflicted or in trouble (Delaney, 1997).

LaBerge and Rheingold (1990) give one more reason why lucid dreaming may not be a desirable option for nightmares. They write that while the majority of lucid dreams are positive, rewarding experiences, some people find the experience of lucid dreaming frightening and, in some cases, extremely disturbing. If a child is frightened with lucid dreaming, then another option should be tried.

Induction Techniques For Lucid Dreaming

There are numerous techniques that can be used to become lucid in dreams. Listed below are several methods that most children should be able to accomplish.

Hypnagogic Technique. A common method of inducing lucid dreams is to fall asleep while focusing on the hypnagogic imagery that accompanies sleep onset. Initially, you are likely to see relatively simple images, flashes of light, geometric patterns, and the like. Gradually more complicated forms appear such as faces, people, and finally entire scenes (LaBerge & Rheingold, 1990).

Just before falling asleep focus on some specific image, any image which may come to you. As soon as you focus on the image, concentrate all of your attention upon it and maintain the concentration for a few minutes, while remaining deeply relaxed. Next, "merge" with the image as you imagine yourself becoming one with it. Eventually allow all of your consciousness to "enter" the image. As you enter the image, you should feel a building sense of momentum, an energy that will pull you completely into the image, through the image and bursting out the other side. At this point you should find yourself in a "whole new world," that is, a whole new dreamscape, which most likely will be a lucid dream. Try flying to launch yourself completely into the lucid state.

Carlos Castaneda's Induction Technique. With this technique, you choose one thing in advance and then find it in your dreams. Castaneda (1973) used his hands because they are always there (in the dreams). Once in the dream you focus on your hands with intent, until they begin to change shape, then you move on to a different object briefly, and then back to your hands. This technique will help attain lucidity. When the dream begins to fade, you can refocus on your hands again to extend the lucid dream.

This technique should be practiced in waking life with the intention of becoming lucid in your dreams. Begin by sitting in a quiet place. Relax your body and mind for several minutes until your mind is clear of all other thoughts. Hold up both of your hands at arms length and focus your gaze on them, intently, yet with relaxation at the same time. Once you have a good visual image of your hands say to yourself, "I see my hands in my dream, I *know* I am dreaming." Repeat this statement to yourself several times, while gazing steadily at your hands. Next, look away at a wall at the far end of the room and neutralize your gaze for several moments by simply focusing on the wall. Return your gaze to your hands again, focus on them steadily and comfortably, and repeat the suggestion as before. Look back at the wall again to neutralize your gaze.

The process of focusing and neutralizing should be repeated five or six times. To help with the induction the first time, the process should be done four or five times a day for a couple of weeks or until the dreamer attains lucidity. Even after the dreamer has experienced lucid dreams this technique can be used as a reminder by focusing on the hands during the day and repeating the suggestion.

Calling in a Dream Helper. A previously established dream figure can be used in establishing lucidity. The figure would be one that is frequently seen in dreams and can be called up in lucid dreams. During a dream, in meditation, while dialoguing, or by some other method, make contact with the dream figure and have it agree to meet you in your next dream and tell you that you are dreaming. Seeing the dream character may then lead to lucidity whenever it is seen (Tholey, 1983).

Fixation. One way of waking yourself up during a frightening dream is by using fixation. Fixation is staring at one object in the dream. For example, if someone is chasing you with a knife, you'd be able to wake yourself up by staring directly at the knife. Find one object or a light in the dream to stare at. The essential thing is to stare directly at one object. This method should always end a dream.

Manipulation Techniques During Lucid Dreaming

Just as lucid dreams can be induced by means of appropriate intentions or autosuggestion methods, so can their contents be influenced. This proves helpful in applying lucid dreaming to some troubling conflict the dreamer is having in waking life. People who go to sleep with their problems on their minds, with the intention of learning something during lucid dreaming, will often be confronted with the conflict. This often leads to important insights that can be of help in the resolution of the problem.

Verbal utterances. You can influence the appearance and behavior of dream figures by addressing them in an appropriate manner. The simple question "Who are you?" can bring about a change in the dream figure. Sometimes figures of strangers are turned into familiar individuals. Tholey (1983) suggests that the dreamer's inner readiness to learn something about the self and the situation, by carrying on a conversation with the dream figure, enables him to expose the disguise of the figure and to achieve the highest level of lucidity in the dream. This lucidity can show what the dream actually symbolizes.

During lucid dreaming other dream characters may possess special abilities. In studies done by Tholey, the subjects were directed to give their dream characters tasks to carry out. Part of the dream figures agreed to carry out the tasks, which included solving simple math problems, writing, rhyming, and speaking in a foreign language. The verbal skills of the dream figures were, in some cases, better than the dreamer's. Tholey suggests that the cognitive abilities of the dream ego and those of the dream figures during lucid dreams should be viewed in connection with distinct cerebral processes.

Establish a target activity. Establishing an activity that you would like to carry out during a lucid dream will help in the intention of becoming lucid. For example, if there is a conflict that you specifically want to work on, then hold that intention in your mind as you are going to sleep. Realizing you are dreaming is exciting, but it can also awaken you, especially if you're not sure what to do next. You should plan in advance something specific to do in the dream. It will also help you to stay lucid for a longer time because you will have an activity on which to focus. Any activity in which the dreamer participates will help sustain the lucidity.

Re-dreaming The Dream

Re-dreaming is another technique that is useful when a child has had a nightmare. Give the child some paper and colored pencils or crayons. Explain to the child that he can change his bad dreams. If he is being chased, the character can be subdued, or a dream-friend can be called in to help. If the child is hurt or sick a dream-doctor can be called on. Ask the child to remember the bad dream and then close his eyes and think about it for a few minutes. While the child still has his eyes closed, ask him what he would like to change about the dream. Explain that he can do whatever he wants in the dream. Tell the child to now change the dream, as he wants it to be, then picture the new dream. Next tell the child to open his eyes and draw the new dream. Explain that all bad dreams can be changed in this way (Garfield, 1984).

LaBerge and Rheingold (1990) give another approach to re-dreaming a nightmare while awake:

1. *Recall and record the nightmare.* If you have had a particular nightmare more than once, recall it in as much detail as you can and write it down. Examine it for points where you could influence the turn of events by doing something differently.

2. *Choose a reentry point and new action.* Choose a specific part of the dream to change, and a specific new action that you would like to try at that point to alter the course of the dream. Also select the most relevant point before the trouble spot at which to reenter the dream. (If it is a long dream, you may wish to begin at the part that immediately precedes the unpleasant events.)

3. *Relax completely.* Find a time and place where you can be alone and uninterrupted for between ten and twenty minutes. In a comfortable position, close your eyes and relax your body completely.

4. *Re-dream the nightmare, seeking resolution.* Beginning at the entry point, you chose in Step 2, imagine you are back in the dream. Visualize the dream happening as it did before until you reach the part at which you have chosen to try a new behavior. See yourself doing the new action, and then continue imagining the dream until you discover what effect your alteration has on its outcome.

5. *Evaluate your re-dreamed resolution.* When the imagined dream has ended, open your eyes. Write down what happened as if it were a normal dream report. Note how you feel about the new dream resolution. If you are not satisfied, and still feel uncomfortable about the dream, try the exercise again with a new alternative action. Achieving a comfortable resolution with the waking exercise may be enough to stop the recurrence of the nightmare.

6. *If the dream recurs, follow your re-dreamed plan of action.* If the dream occurs again, do in the dream what you visualized during waking reentry. Remember that the dream cannot harm you and be firmly resolved to carry through with your new behavior.

Imagery Rehearsal Therapy

Imagery rehearsal is a way of battling nightmares where the dreamer chooses a new ending. This therapy has proven beneficial for people who have the same recurring nightmares over a period of time. Instead of interpreting the dream, a new ending is chosen. Once the dreamer has the new ending, she takes some time while awake to imagine the new ending over and over again. Usually the new ending is practiced in 10- to 20-minute daily practice sessions (Barrett, 1996).

Imagery therapy is also good for people who have Chronic Nightmare Disorder, which is characterized as:
- Disturbing or unpleasant dreams at least every week or every month.
- Sleep is disturbed by bad dreams.
- Anxiety and fear about going to sleep due to concern about having a bad dream.
- Symptoms have lasted six months or longer.

Imagery rehearsal is a more active approach to nightmares. Instead of interpreting dreams and dissecting their symbolic meaning, nightmare therapy uses the dreams to help decrease chronic nightmares, improve sleep quality, and decrease posttraumatic symptom severity. The imagery rehearsal technique teaches the dreamer how to literally change his nightmares while he is still awake, so that he will actually gain greater control and more conscious control over them. The technique is described in the following steps:
1. The dreamer should be in a quiet and relaxed state of mind.
2. While awake, the dreamer works out a new ending for his disturbing dream. For example, escaping from an attacker.
3. Also while awake, the dreamer rehearses the new ending again and again.
4. The dreamer then applies the concept of the new dream ending to real life situations, such as standing up to a bully.
5. Nightmares fade.

Treatment For Anxiety Disorders

As stated earlier, anxiety disorders may be a large cause of nightmares. Anxiety disorders of childhood may continue into adolescence and young adulthood, first leading to maladaptive avoidance behavior and later to increasingly idiosyncratic thinking and behavior. Typically, however, this is not the case. As affected children grow and have wider interactions in school and in peer-group activities, they are likely to benefit from such corrective experiences as making friends and succeeding at given tasks. Teachers have become more and more aware of the needs of both overanxious and shy, withdrawn children and of ways to help them foster constructive interpersonal relationships (Carson, 1992).

Behavior therapy procedures, used in structured group experiences within educational settings, can often help speed up and ensure favorable outcomes. Such procedures include assertiveness training, help with mastering essential competencies, and desensitization. This last procedure may be limited in its application to young children, however, for a number of reasons, including the inability of young children to relax while imagining emotionally charged stimuli. With children, desensitization procedures must be explicitly tailored to a particular problem, and in vivo methods (using graded real-life situations) may be more effective than the use of imagined situations. For example, Carson cites the following treatment that was successful in the case of six-year-old, Romeo, who showed pathological anxiety when he was separated from his mother. The treatment included the following procedures:

1. Exposure of the child to a graded series of situations involving the actual fear-arousing stimulus - that is, separation from the mother for increasingly longer intervals.
2. Use of food during these separations as an anxiety inhibitor - which might involve taking the child to the hospital cafeteria for something to eat [where the therapy was taking place].
3. Instruction of the parents on how to reduce the child's excessive dependence on the mother - for example, through letting him learn to do things for himself.

After ten consecutive sessions, Romeo's separation anxiety was reduced to the point that he could stay home with a competent babysitter for an hour and then for increasingly longer periods. During the summer, he was enrolled in a vacation church school, which he enjoyed; when the new semester began at public school, he entered the first grade and made an adequate adjustment. It should be emphasized that the cooperation of the parents - particularly the mother - was a key factor in the treatment.

Posttraumatic Stress Disorder.

Supportive therapy and proper rest (induced by sedatives if necessary) usually can alleviate symptoms that lead to posttraumatic stress disorder. Repetitive talking about the experience and constantly reliving it in fantasies or nightmares may serve as built-in repair mechanisms to help an individual adjust to the traumatic event. Horowitz (1969) stated:

"A traumatic perceptual experience remains in some special form of memory storage until it is mastered. Before mastery, vivid sensory images of the experiences tend to intrude into consciousness and may evoke unpleasant emotions. Through such repetitions the images, ideas, and associated affects may be worked through progressively. Thereafter, the images lose their intensity and the tendency toward repetition of the experience loses its motive force" (p. 552).

Fear Of The Dark

A fear of the dark is natural; it's a basic instinct and one of the most common fears of children. Fear of the dark tends to wax and wane as a child's understanding of the world develops. For example, while a preschooler might be afraid of the dark because she thinks there is a monster under the bed, an eight-year-old who understands that monsters don't exist may be frightened that a burglar will break into the house during the night. A child's fear of the dark should not be belittled.

126

If a child is afraid, the parent can ask the child what he is feeling when he's alone in the dark. Even if his apprehension seems foolish to the parent, he should be reassured with concrete information. For example, if the child hears noises, the parent can explain that the house does make funny noises at night. Then the parent and child can listen together and identify all the noises, such as the furnace coming on or water running through the pipes.

Many children will ask to have their bedroom light left on because of this fear. The dark, however, is not dangerous. By leaving the child's light turned on, the parent may actually be telling the child that the dark is dangerous. Being in a dark room should be comforting and soothing, not stressful (Pearce, 1999). The parent can teach the child to calm himself by saying, "I'm safe in the dark, my mom and dad are nearby" or "That sound was just the heat coming on."

Children who have always slept in a darkened room, usually won't be afraid of the dark. However, if the child is having nightmares, that may be causing the fear. Parents can help the child overcome the fear. Begin by gradually decreasing the light in the room, starting with a lower-watt bulb in the lamp, then leaving a light on only in the hallway. The parent should offer praise each time the child goes to sleep with less light. The parent should also make sure that pre-sleep activities are beneficial for good sleeping.

<u>When To Seek Help For Nightmares</u>

Moderate nightmare activity may be a potentially healthy sign that the unconscious mind is actively coping with stress and change. Frequent nightmares may indicate unresolved conflicts that are overwhelming the child. When children's nightmares persist, when the content is consistently violent or disturbing, or when the upsetting conflicts in the dreams never seem to change or even achieve partial resolution, it may be time to seek further help from a mental health specialist or pediatrician. This is so especially, if there is no obvious stress in the child's life. Repetitive nightmares could also be caused by a reaction to drugs or a physical condition, so it is advisable to consult a physician to rule out medical causes when nightmares do not appear to have a psychological origin.

Repetitive nightmares are often accompanied by other symptoms, especially fears of going to sleep, anxieties or phobias. Increased nightmares can usually be linked to a recognizable stress in the child's life such as absence or loss of a parent, suffering abuse or violence, marital or custody disputes in the family. Social or academic difficulties at school, such as being teased or having an undiagnosed learning or attention problem, can also increase nightmares.

Siegel and Bulkeley (1999) say that nightmares are more often like a vaccine than a poison. A vaccination infects us with a minute dose of a disease that mobilizes our antibodies and makes us more resistant to the virulence of smallpox or polio. As distressing as nightmares can be, they offer powerful information about issues that are distressing the child. When children share their nightmares and receive reassurance from their parents, they feel the emotional sting of the dream, but also begin the process of strengthening their psychological defenses and facing their fears with more resilience. Gradually, a parent's empathic response to the child's nightmares can break the cycle of bad dreams and transform intensely negative experiences into triumphs of assertiveness and collaborative family problem-solving.

Chapter 10
Getting a Good Night's Sleep

We have seen that dreaming is important for a person's overall wellbeing, and getting a good night's sleep is important for dreaming. While we are sleeping, our dreams are restoring our psychological balance, keeping us mentally oriented, and allowing us to explore new avenues not always available in waking life. Studies have shown that a person who has been deprived of dreaming for a short period of time will be tense and irritable during the day, and after an extended period of time, the person will likely become mentally unbalanced (Krippner & Hughes, 1970). While Dement (1960) was conducting a study on dream deprivation, some of his subjects actually quit because the stress on them was so high. One subject left in a state of panic.

Sleep can't be turned on or off at will, it is a habit and one of the first routines children need to develop. However, about 1 in 3 children under the age of 5 have disturbed sleep; and of these, almost a third have a serious problem. As children grow older, their sleep improves. By the age of 8, only 1 child in 10 has sleep problems (Pearce, 1999).

<u>What Is Sleep</u>

Sleep is very important on every level. Sleep is nourishment, it allows us to rebuild our bodies and brains. Sleep also serves a function related to memory and learning. Sleep helps us make connections between recent and old memories and helps us "tie up loose ends." Sleep is a state necessary for restoration. For example, it gives the body a chance to repair muscles and other tissues and replaces aging or dead cells.

Too little sleep can blunt our reactions, affect our ability to perform, and hinder making decisions. It can also affect our mood and behavior and make us irritable during the next day. Sleep is important because it allows the body to replenish its reserves. It's a key to our health and wellbeing just as eating and drinking is. Growth hormone in children is secreted during sleep and so are chemicals that are important to our immune system. Weakening the body's immune system can make us more susceptible to colds, flu and other infectious diseases.

We spend close to one-third of our lives in sleep. Sleep releases the mind from the ordinary strictures of society and the inner restrictions of our conscience. It is not a state of inactivity, but there is a very different organization of our bodies and brain. A great deal is happening while we sleep. In our dreams, we are conscious; we see and often hear, feel, and experience things. But it is a different way than when we are awake. We live a different life in our dreams. We are using the same brain, the same equipment, as during waking consciousness, but it's activity is organized in a different manner (Hartmann, 1987).

The body itself is not inactive, but simply differently organized during sleep. For instance, our delicately tuned breathing apparatus is something of which we are not usually even aware. It breathes for us while we are doing something else. But when we analyze it in detail, it turns out that each breath depends on impulses that are sent out from the brain stem to the diaphragm and the chest, initiating inspiration; and then other impulses are sent out for expiration. At the same time, impulses are sent to the muscles in the back of our throat to ensure that the airway is open. Certain sensors tell us that we have too little oxygen or too much carbon dioxide in our blood, that the air passages are not fully open, and so on. It turns out that all these delicate mechanisms are organized differently during sleep and during wakefulness.

Sleep is a behavioral state, a regularly recurrent normal behavioral state, characterized by relative inactivity and a great increase in response threshold to the environment; that is, it takes a louder noise or greater stimulation to produce any reaction in a sleeping person than in one who is awake. This behavioral state is also associated with a biological state, a state of the brain characterized by decreased activity in some areas and increased activity in certain other areas (Hartmann, 1987).

Stages of sleep. During sleep onset, breathing and pulse slow down slightly. There are usually a few body movements and sometimes slow movements of the eyes. During this time, the brain waves, the rhythmic electrical activity produced by the brain, undergo a number of changes. Recordings on an electroencephalogram (EEG) show that the mixture of ten-per-second activity (alpha waves) and high-frequency waves that characterizes wakefulness gradually gives way to a pattern of mixed low-voltage activity known as stage 1 sleep – a transitional state. During stage 1, you began to feel drowsy and are semi-conscious as you fall asleep.

130

This is followed by a state characterized by sleep spindles - groups of fast waves, thirteen or fifteen per second, which are basically seen only during sleep – and certain spiking waves known as K-complexes. These spindles and K-complexes characterize what is called stage 2 of sleep. Stage 2 is the first stage that everyone recognizes as "definite" sleep. During stage 2 you gradually fall into a deeper unconscious state.

In the next few minutes in a healthy sleeper, the EEG activity slows down a bit so that there are more and more slow waves. (Slow waves, or delta waves, have a frequency of one-half to four per second.) This is referred to as stage 3 sleep, when at least 20 percent of the record is taken up by slow waves.

After approximately twenty to thirty minutes of stage 3 sleep the sleeper falls into stage 4, or slow-wave sleep. Stage 4 of sleep is when at least 50 percent of the record is taken up by slow waves. This is the deepest level of sleep. After approximately ninety minutes of stage 4 sleep, the pattern of brain waves suddenly changes into what appears as a burst of activity even more lively than that recorded during waking hours.

What happens is that the sleeper, after one to two hours of stage 2, stage 3, and stage 4 sleep, seems to have a lightening of sleep; there are a few body movements, and the EEG record resembles stage 1 sleep, the lightest stage. At this same time, a number of other changes occur: the eyes begin to move together, sometimes quite rapidly, and you enter a state known as rapid-eye-movement sleep, or REM sleep. Everything changes somewhat during this time: respiration becomes somewhat faster and definitely more irregular; the same is true of pulse and blood pressure.

Various studies report that from 50 to 90 percent of the time, sleepers can describe dreams after awakenings from REM sleep. REM sleep is also known as dreaming sleep. Dreams are sometimes reported from other parts of the night, too, but they are less frequent and less dramatic. These periods of REM sleep occur four or five times during a typical night. Sleepers alternate between non-REM sleep and REM sleep approximately every ninety or one hundred minutes during the night. REM periods increase in length as the night progresses and take up a total of perhaps one-fourth of a night, while non-REM sleep (stages 2, 3, and 4) takes up the other three-fourths of the night (Hartmann, 1987).

REM. During stage 4 sleep you move about and some people even sleep-walk, but during REM sleep your body undergoes "sleep paralysis." Your whole body is paralyzed apart from your chest, to allow you to breathe, and your eyes, which do not stop moving. Researchers believe that paralysis occurs during the dreaming phase of sleep in order to prevent you from acting out your dreams and harming yourself (Spurr, 1999).

Unborn babies do not experience sleep paralysis, and scientists believe that this is because nature "knows" the baby is completely protected in the womb. In fact, when pregnant women feel their baby moving, the baby may well be dreaming. Many scientists believe that during their dream phases, the unborn babies are processing what they can hear from inside the womb. Newborn infants scream out sometimes when asleep as though having a nightmare. Babies experience a huge amount of REM time that diminishes with age.

According to Gackenbach & Bosveld (1989), the function of REM sleep is to integrate new information with the old. "It is an unedited creator that is forever weaving new stories without worrying whether the plot is realistic or the characters believable. Our dreams are new worlds spun by the muse that resides in each of us" (p. 61). Our waking lives are often so busy living our lives that we forget about the part of us that creates. Our dreams allow us to be storytellers and mythmakers.

The REM state is necessary for the optimal maintenance of the personality and new learning (Rossi, 1971). Through self-reflection and self-awareness we can change our behavior. Studies have shown that students studying for exams spend more time than usual in REM sleep. Intellectually gifted children seem to engage in more REM sleep than other children, whereas mentally handicapped children engage in less (Goodale, 1994).

REM sleep is basically a process for "programming" the brain. This programming system is homeostatic, organizing and storing memories (perceptual, cognitive, and behavioral). This explains why newborns need more REM time than adults to develop their central nervous systems (Krippner & Hughes, 1970).

Studies done by Foulkes (1982) show that the dream content of children and adolescents appears to be mostly about play and recreational activities. Dreams of play appear to represent extensions of the child's waking ego impulses to exploration and manipulation of his environment. The REM state can thus be understood as a period during which internal programs are being synthesized so that they can later be actualized in the behavior involved in the exploration and manipulation of the child's environment.

Sleep Disorders

Since sleep occupies one-third of our lives and consists of two states, the possibilities for disorders of sleep can be numerous. The control of the body's physiological functions is totally different during sleep than during wakefulness and sometimes differs even between the two major sleep states, REM sleep and non-REM sleep. Those differences provide an opportunity for many specific disorders of the sleep mechanisms to appear, and also result in the possibility of secondary disorders. For example, various chemical and environmental stimuli may have different effects during sleep than they do during wakefulness and may, thus, unexpectedly produce sleep disorders.

How does a person know if the condition needs treatment? The important issue is not so much what happens at night but what happens during the day. The person needs help if the sleep disorder appears to be producing problems during waking life - problems in interacting with other people, with school work, or feeling good during the day. It's important to see how well the person functions during the day (Hartmann, 1987). There are many sleep disorders; the following are ones that may be relevant to children.

Arousal Disorders. Arousal disorders are episodic events that arouse the sleeper, usually within two hours of sleep onset. The best studied of these include sleepwalking, night terrors, and enuresis, or bed-wetting. All three conditions are most common in childhood. It has been estimated that at least 20 percent of children at ages five to seven have at least a few episodes of sleepwalking, night terrors, or enuresis. These conditions remain fairly common in adolescence and young adulthood but then decrease steadily with age (Hartmann, 1987).

Sleepwalking. Sleepwalking disorder usually begins between the ages of 6 and 12. The symptoms involve repeated episodes in which the person leaves his bed and walks around without being conscious of the experience or remembering it later. It is estimated that 1 to 6 percent of children experience regular or periodic sleepwalking episodes. Children with this problem normally go to sleep in the usual manner but arise during the second or third hour of sleep. They may walk to another room of the house or even outside, and they may engage in complex activities. Finally they return to bed and in the morning remember nothing that has taken place.

While moving about, sleepwalkers' eyes are partially or fully open; they avoid obstacles, listen when spoken to, and ordinarily respond to commands, such as return to bed. Shaking them will usually awaken sleepwalkers, and they will be surprised and perplexed at finding themselves in an unexpected place. Sleepwalking episodes usually last from 15 to 30 minutes. The causes of sleepwalking are not fully understood. Studies have shown that sleepwalking takes place during NREM (non-rapid eye movement) sleep, but its relationship to dreaming remains unclear. In general, it appears that sleepwalking is related to some anxiety-arousing situation that has just occurred or is expected to occur in the near future (Carson, 1992).

Sleepwalking is obvious to an observer, though not always to the sleepwalker. Technically, one does not have to actually walk around to qualify as a sleepwalker. Some people simply stand up or sit in bed or roll over and strike out in flailing motions without quite knowing it. Attempts to restrain a sleepwalker are often met with resistance. Sleepwalkers can experience emotional distress and embarrassment because of their nighttime activities, keeping them from staying with friends or vacationing. Sleepwalking usually occurs early in the night and arises from stage 3 or stage 4 sleep. There is a deeper (slower) brain wave pattern of sleeping than dreaming, deeper than REM sleep.

Dr. John Pearce (1999), recommends the following suggestions if your child is having an episode of sleepwalking:

- Do not wake the child. Lead the child back to bed and make sure he settles. Tuck the child in and say your regular nighttime phrase.
- Check to be sure there aren't any obstacles for him to fall over. Your child's safety is the most important thing.
- If it happens regularly, make a chart and see if there is a particular pattern behind the sleepwalking.

Night Terrors. Night terrors consist of episodes of screaming in terror followed by an awakening with no recall of a dream, or occasionally a recall of a single frightening image: "Something is sitting on me," or, "Something is closing in on me." In the sleep laboratory, it shows that these episodes of night terrors, like those of sleepwalking, occur out of stage 3 or stage 4 sleep early during the sleep period. They are associated with tremendous increases of pulse rate, respiratory rate, and blood pressure during the thirty seconds or so it takes to wake up (Hartmann, 1987).

Enuresis. Enuresis, the involuntary passage of urine during the night, is most common in children; this condition, too, is found to occur during periods of stage 3 and stage 4 sleep early in the night. It occurs somewhat more frequently in people who have night terrors and/or sleepwalking as well.

All three of these conditions - sleepwalking, night terrors, and enuresis - usually run in families to a certain extent. They are called disorders of arousal, since they are not ongoing processes, such as dreams, that would be interrupted by an arousal; rather, the condition is the unusual arousal experience itself. These three conditions are usually relatively harmless, and don't need specific treatment.

Sleep Deprivation. Sleep deprivation can cause mind-mood changes such as irritability, sadness, lack of motivation, poor concentration and a reduction in short-term memory. People who are experiencing sleep deprivation or broken sleep may crash in the middle of an activity (such as reading). These "microsleeps" - tiny, often imperceptible periods of crashing, are the body's way of taking matters into its own hands.

Sleep deprivation can also cause changes in blood pressure, heart and respiratory rates, nystagmus (darting of the eyes), slurred speech, hand tremors, increased pain sensitivity and hyperactive reflexes. The person's skin may look pasty with dark circles under the eyes, and they may slouch. Shivering may occur as a result of having difficulty regulating body temperature.

Children need at least eight or nine hours of sleep every night in order to function at optimal levels. When children are consistently sleep deprived, it not only affects their health, but also makes it harder for them to control their behavior. These children often show signs of attention deficit disorder (ADD), have trouble focusing, and become more fidgety.

Sleep Paralysis. Sleep paralysis is a condition in which one is "half awake" in the sense of the mind being awake but the muscles refuse to move. It's when REM sleep intrudes into waking hours. Almost everyone has occasionally had a brief episode of sleep paralysis. It can seem like a terrifying experience, but is actually quite harmless. However, if it continues for more than a few seconds, it may be a sign of narcolepsy.

REM Behavior Disorder. REM behavior disorder causes some people to act out their dreams. Usually we can't move during dreams because our muscles are actively paralyzed. People with this disorder show all the normal signs of sleeping except the loss of muscle tone. This can lead to odd behavior, such as a man getting into his car, driving down the road, then waking up wondering what's going on (Nadis, 1994).

There is often vivid, action-filled, violent dreams, that the dreamer acts out, sometimes resulting in injury to the dreamer or the sleeping partner. Although similar to sleepwalking, REM behavior disorder is not an arousal disorder, which sleepwalking is. Also, sleepwalking occurs during non-rapid eye movement, is episodic and is usually triggered by stress. REM behavior disorder is organic and can be treated with medication. It may be an early indication of narcolepsy (Pagel, 2000).

Narcolepsy. Narcolepsy consists primarily of attacks of irresistible sleepiness in the daytime. The person typically falls asleep suddenly while watching television or sitting in a classroom. In severe cases, attacks occur while engaged in an important activity, such as driving. Narcoleptics go directly into REM sleep, often having strange dreams that will wake them up. Nighttime sleep may be fragmented with frequent wakenings. It is thought that in narcolepsy, there is a commingling of the three states of being: awake, REM sleep, and non-REM sleep (Nadis, 1994). Associated symptoms may include cataplexy, hypnogogic hallucinations, and sleep paralysis, though they may not always be present.

Cataplexy is characterized by sudden loss of muscle tone and collapse (or partial collapse) during wakefulness. Sometimes the person remains conscious; sometimes there is a brief loss of consciousness associated with the experience of dreaming. A strong emotion such as anger sometimes precipitates an attack of cataplexy. Hypnogogic hallucinations may occur while falling asleep or occasionally while waking up (hypnopomic); the person has a kind of hallucination in which he sees someone else in the room or hears someone calling his name. The hallucination passes very quickly, and the person is then sure that no one was really there.

Narcolepsy runs in families to a certain extent. Most often, it begins around the age of 15 or 20 and is thereafter a lifelong condition. A number of treatments are available for narcolepsy, usually consisting of using a stimulant medication such as Ritalin in the daytime. In some cases, especially when cataplexy is present, other medications are required also. The disturbing "accessory symptoms" such as cataplexy and sleep paralysis almost always improve or cease with the proper medication. In some cases, narcolepsy can be treated without medication by carefully spacing naps during the day to relieve the excessive sleepiness (Hartmann, 1987).

When should narcolepsy be suspected? A person should be checked for narcolepsy if:
- She often feels excessively and overwhelmingly sleepy during the day, even after having a full night's sleep.
- She falls asleep when she's not intending to, such as while having dinner, talking, driving, or working.
- She collapses suddenly or her neck muscles feel too weak to hold her head up when she laughs, becomes angry, surprised, or shocked.
- She finds herself briefly unable to talk or move while falling asleep or waking up.

Sleep Apnea. Sleep apnea is a condition in which breathing stops a number of times during the night. The control of respiration is considerably different during sleep than it is during wakefulness. Recordings demonstrate that in some people, airflow (air entering or leaving the nose or mouth) simply stops - not just a few times but in severe cases several hundred times during the night. Luckily, reflex mechanisms wake us up when oxygen levels become too low or carbon dioxide levels too high, so breathing stops usually for only ten to thirty seconds. An arousal quickly follows, during which the person starts to breathe again.

The mechanisms producing sleep apnea are complex, but basically there are two major ways that airflow can stop. With central sleep apnea, the neurons of the central nervous system responsible for sending out impulses to the respiratory muscles simply do not function or do not function adequately. Central sleep apnea,

136

is seen in infants in whom the mechanisms in the brain, responsible for regulating sleep, have not yet developed fully.

In obstructive sleep apnea, the breathing muscles in the diaphragm and chest continue to function, but something blocks the flow of air through the throat. Sometimes this is simply fatty tissue in someone who is overweight; sometimes the blockage involves a tumor or other disease condition in the throat. But often the blockage seems to be caused by an improper opening of the posterior pharynx (back of the throat) so that air does not get through properly with each breath. In this last instance, obstructive and central apnea are not so different since neuromuscular problems affecting nerve impulses to the throat muscles can produce an obstruction of the throat and, thus, obstructive apnea (Hartmann, 1987).

Although sleep apnea is a rare condition for children, it is important to recognize because it causes problems for the child during the daytime. Common symptoms of obstructive sleep apnea include: snoring, breath holding while asleep, restlessness, mouth breathing, sleepiness during the day, insomnia, difficult, irritable behavior, and hyperactivity. Obstructive sleep apnea may be caused by airway obstruction; for example, tonsils and adenoids, obesity, blocked nose, or parental smoking. Medical attention should be attained if you believe your child suffers from sleep apnea (Pearce, 1999).

Insomnia. Of all the symptoms associated with sleep disorders, insomnia is the most common. Insomnia is manifested by any one or more of a group of related complaints: trouble falling asleep, staying awake for hours, trouble remaining asleep, waking up during the night and waking up too early. All of these together constitute insomnia.

Insomnia consists of two different and usually separable symptoms: difficulty in falling asleep and difficulty in remaining asleep. Difficulty in falling asleep is very common in young people. Insomnia can result from a variety of medical and psychological causes as well as insufficient daytime activity and poor sleep hygiene

Nocturnal Myoclonus. Nocturnal myoclonus consists of involuntary jerking movements of the arms and legs. The person may wake up frequently every night or may not notice anything much except waking up tired or being tired during the day. It's an experience of non-restorative sleep. Nocturnal myoclonus is more common in females. Often there will be strange bits of dreams upon awakening. Sometimes there will be very active dreams such as jumping or running.

Most people experience nocturnal myoclonus occasionally while falling asleep but if it happens a lot and interferes with sleep something could be wrong.

137

In that case it would be important to get information from an observer. Do the legs jerk for long periods of time? Does the whole body jerk? In laboratory testing, muscle jerking can be seen every thirty to sixty seconds for hours, sometimes throughout the night. Nocturnal myoclonus is one of the underlying causes of insomnia and of daytime sleepiness. Sometimes it accompanies other conditions, such as sleep apnea and it can occasionally be a side effect of various medications (Hartmann, 1987).

Bruxism. Bruxism is nocturnal teeth grinding. This condition is usually not noticed by the sleeper but is evident to anyone nearby. It is a fairly common disorder that involves grinding the teeth powerfully during the night, making a loud noise - often loud enough to wake up someone else in the room, though the sleeper doesn't hear it. There is a familial tendency towards bruxism; that is, it tends to run in families. Bruxism can occur at any age but is more common in older children than the very young.

Bruxism seems to be more common in people who are somewhat tense or angry. It is usually worse when the person is undergoing tense, stressful situations. There is some indication that bruxism occurs especially in people with suppressed anger - feelings of anger for which one has no adequate outlet. Some people cause serious damage to their teeth and gums by the constant grinding.

Help For Insomnia

Sleep Hygiene. If a person has insomnia, it doesn't necessarily mean that they need treatment. Instead, the person can try solving the problem by increasing sleep hygiene. The following suggestions can be tried out until a solution is found (Hartmann, 1987):
- Go to bed at a regular time each night.
- Get up at approximately the same time each morning.
- Eat meals at regular times.
- Exercise at regular times (moderate, regular exercise two to four hours before bedtime is especially helpful).
- Sleep in a darkened room.
- Eliminate noise in the sleeping area.
- Use a mattress that is neither too soft nor too hard.
- Avoid using uncomfortable pillows.
- Be sure the room is free of known allergens.
- Adjust the temperature to be the most comfortable for you.
- Drinking a glass of warm milk can be of help in falling asleep.

Medication. Another frequent cause of insomnia is prescribed medication. There are hardly any drugs that do not have some kind of side effects, and sleep problems are common. There are hundreds of drugs, so it is best to always check the warning labels to see what to expect. Some of the most common drugs that cause insomnia include those that have a stimulant effect such as amphetamines (Dexedrine, Eskatrol), methylphenidate (Ritalin, used in the treatment of ADD), pemoline (Cylert), and many similar drugs used to treat narcolepsy and sometimes obesity.

Some drugs only have a stimulant in certain people such as those used as antidepressants. Caffeine is the world's most widely used mild stimulant and can interfere with sleep. If children drink a lot of soft drinks loaded with caffeine in the evening, they may be bouncing off the walls by bedtime. The drinks with the highest levels of caffeine include coffee, soft drinks and hot chocolate.

Even drugs known as sleeping pills or tranquilizers can induce insomnia. The problem is that there is usually always a rebound effect in the opposite direction when the medication is stopped. A period of mild and sometimes severe insomnia after withdrawal is expectable, though people's reaction vary. Some people hardly notice it and other people have trouble sleeping for weeks afterward.

<u>Psychological causes.</u> Insufficient physical or mental activity can cause a person to have trouble falling asleep. It's hard to fall asleep if you are just not tired, especially if the person naps frequently during the day. Just the opposite may be true for some children in that when they become too tired, they become irritable and fussy and "too tired to fall asleep."

Sleeping too much for several days or weeks can also cause a problem. Some people sleep a lot as a way of avoiding stressful situations. It's a way of shutting out the world. This condition is known as transient psychophysiological insomnia. The sleep disturbance produced can be either difficulty in falling asleep or frequent waking during the night and an inability to get back to sleep. In younger people, it is usually difficulty in falling asleep (Hartmann, 1987).

Oversleeping may result in temporary insomnia. Depression especially may cause someone to experience hypersomnia - excessive sleep, rather than lack of sleep. In these cases, the person sleeps for longer and longer periods of time. The onset is often imperceptible - there is no definite starting point - but sleeping troubles seem to become worse over a period of months. This is common in teenagers.

Anxiety can clearly produce difficulty in sleeping. Worry over an upcoming event, such as a school project, a test, or speaking in front of a group of people. Grieving over the loss of a loved one is a common cause of insomnia and a normal part of the grieving process. If a child has frequent nightmares, there may be a fear of going to sleep, afraid there will be another nightmare. There is often anxiety about moving to a new neighborhood, parents getting divorced, health problems, or experiencing new situations. The list is endless. Most of these causes are temporary, however, if the situation continues for a long period of time it is advised to seek help.

Dreams, as already stated, are judged in different ways for various people. For, given the same dream, there is one interpretation for a king, another for his subjects; one for a warrior, another for a farmer; one for a noble, another for a poor man; one for a man, another for a woman.

—Achmet - Greek philosopher in the tenth century

Conclusion

The most amazing things about dreams are their infinite creativity, variety and availability. There are many benefits to remembering dreams. By accepting our dream experiences, there is usually an increase in self-acceptance, changes in awareness, and attitudes about the self. By learning to face our fears *during* dreams, we can develop a sturdier approach to daily life. By actively relating to our dreams, instead of ignoring them or uselessly worrying about them, we can improve our quality of life.

Dream recall on its own is not as beneficial as working with our dreams. Many of the images in dreams cannot be found in any dream dictionary, no matter how comprehensive. Our dream images are formed from personal experience and that makes them unique. In the case of children, the content is portrayed more symbolically. When the children are able to reflect and elaborate on their own waking experiences, then their dreams will reflect their own self-expression.

The only person who can really interpret a dream is the dreamer himself. A guide can help elicit the meaning of a dream from the dreamer's unconscious, however, that brings in to play the guide's own personality and prejudices. The person who created the dream did so using a part of his own mind, although once awake it's not always easy to access. There are many ways to regain access and jog the mind.

During dreams, we enter a world of timeless reality. We all experience communication from our higher selves during our nightly dream states. Our dreams also guide us on the path that leads towards a better understanding of our life's purpose. As our personal healer, our dreams, even our nightmares can diagnose and heal us at many levels even if we don't understand them. Exploring nightmares can help uncover hidden fears, reveal inner sources of personal power, and help us express our emotions.

Exploration of our dreams can lead us to better sleep and a healthier and more satisfying waking life. Dreams always come in the service of wholeness and health. We can use them for self-improvement, insight, and creative expression.

Dreams are a way to learn new skills, explore new behaviors, and make changes in our lives.

Working with children and their dreams can lead to signposts of the kinds of problems they may be having in waking life. Working together can also lead to a closer, warmer relationship between the child and parent. Exploring children's dreams with them is one way in which the parent can help nurture the development of the child's personality. Exploring dreams together can also provide encouragement and the inspiration for the introduction of new or creative pursuits, such as writing or artwork.

As adults we can learn much about the nature of our children from the nature of their dreams. Our purpose is to encourage our children to realize they have inner resources, to encourage the ones that already exist, and to point out others that are available to them.

Appendix A

This list is a sampling of the drugs that can cause nightmares.

Drug	Drug Use	Drug	Drug Use
Ambien	Insomnia	Clonidine	Hypertension
Acebutolol	Hypertension	Desipramine	Depression
Adapin	Depression, anxiety, posttraumatic stress disorder, sleep disorders, chronic pain	Desyrel	Depression
Amitriptyline	Depression	Doxepin	Depression, anxiety
Amoxapine	Depression	Elavil	Depression, pain, anxiety, insomnia
Atenolol	Hypertension	Ethchlorvynol	Insomnia
Bisoprolol	Hypertension	Fluoxetine	Depression
Buspar	Anxiety disorders	Halofantrene	Malaria
Carbidopa-levodopa	Parkinson	Hydroxyxorquine	Malaria
Carteolol	Hypertension	Lariam	Malaria prevention and treatment
Catapres	Hypertension, ADD	Propoxyphene	Pain
Chloral hydrate	Insomnia	Propranolol	Hypertension, migraine
Ciprofloxacin	Antibiotic	Prozac	Depression, bulimia, obsessive-compulsive disorder, anorexia, migraine, panic disorder

Appendix B

Children's reading list for nightmare help. This list is an example of the multitude of books for children on this subject.

There's A Nightmare In My Closet, by Mercer Mayer
There's A Monster Under My Bed, by James Howe
We Are Monsters, by Mary Packard
The Dream Eater, by Christian Garrison
Junie B. Jones Has A Monster Under Her Bed, by Barbara Park
Tell Me Something Happy Before I Go To Sleep, by Joyce Dunbar
The Berenstain Bears And The Bad Dream, by Stan and Jan Berenstain
The Berenstain Bears In The Dark, by Stan and Jan Berenstain
One Dark And Scary Night, by Bill Cosby
Go Away, Big Green Monster!, by Ed Emberley
Glad Monster Sad Monster, by Ed Emberly and Anne Miranda

There are several book series that can help children with the trials and tribulations of childhood. Listed below are a few of these series.

It's OK!, by Beth Robbins, prepares children for new experiences.
Books in the series:

Tom's Afraid Of The Dark
Tom and Ally Visit the Doctor
Tom, Ally, and the New Baby
Tom's First Day at School
Tom, Ally, and the Babysitter
Tom's New Haircut

Let's Talk About, by Joy Berry, explains to the child how to handle even the toughest situations and emotions.
Books included in the series:

Feeling Afraid
Feeling Angry
Saying No
Feeling Sad
Being Helpful
Needing Attention

Mister Rogers' First Experience Books, by Fred Rogers.
Books included in the series:

Going to the Hospital
When a Pet Dies
The New Baby
Making Friends

I'm Safe!, by Wendy Gordon.
Books include:

I'm Safe! From monsters
I'm Safe! With the New Baby
I'm Safe! In the water
I'm Safe! On my bike
I'm Safe! With My Pet
I'm Safe! At the Mall
I'm Safe! In the Car

Appendix C

Children's reading list of books dealing with medical problems.
This is a partial list of the multitude of books for children on this subject.

Madeline, by Ludwig Bemelmans

The Lion Who Had Asthma, by Jonathan London

I've Got Chicken Pox, by True Kelley

My Doctor, Harlow Rockwell

Robby Visits the Doctor, by Martine Davison

Maggie and the Emergency Room, by Martine Davison

Rita Goes to the Hospital, by Martine Davison

A Trip to the Doctor, by Margot Linn and Catherine Siracusa

When Mommy is Sick, by Ferne Sherkin-Langer

List of adult books on preparing children for hospitalization:

Emotional Care of Hospitalized Children, by Madeline Petrillo and Sirgay Sanger

Between Parent and Child, by Haim Ginott

Windows to Our Children: A Gestalt Therapy Approach to Children and Adolescents, by Violet Oaklander

Effects of Hospitalization on Children, by Evelyn K. Oremland

Stress and Coping in Child Health, by Annette La Greca (Ed.)

Anxiety in Children, by Ved P. Varma (Ed.)

Prepare for Surgery Heal Faster: A Guide of Mind-Body Techniques, by Peggy Huddleston

References

Achterberg, J. "Imagery and Medicine: Psychophysiological Speculations." *Journal of Mental Imagery*, 8, 1-14., 1984.

Avila, E. *Woman Who Glows in the Dark.* New York: Jeremy P. Tarcher/Putnam, 1999.

Barrett, D. *Trauma and Dreams.* Cambridge: Harvard University Press, 2001.

Baylis, J. *Sleep On It! The Practical Side of Dreaming.* Marina del Rey: DeVorss & Company, 1977.

Browne, S. *Sylvia Browne's Book of Dreams.* New York: Dutton, 2002.

Campbell, R. *Kids in Danger: Disarming the Destructive Power of Anger in Your Child.* Colorado Springs: Chariot Victor Publishing, 1999.

Carson, R. *Abnormal Psychology and Modern Life,* ninth ed. New York: HarperCollins Publishers Inc., 1992.

Cartwright, R. D., Lloyd, S., Knight, S., & Trenholme, I. "Broken Dreams: A Study of the Effects of Divorce and Depression on Dream Content." *Psychiatry,* 47, 251-259, 1984.

Cartwright, R. D. "'Masochism' in Dreaming and Its Relationship to Depression." *Dreaming,* 2, 79-84, 1992.

Castaneda, C. *Journey to Ixtlan: The Lessons of Don Juan.* New York: Simon and Schuster, 1973.

Chetwynd, T. *How to Interpret Your Own Dreams (In One Minute or Less).* New York: P. H. Wyden, 1980.

Delaney, G. *Living Your Dreams.* San Francisco: Harper & Row, 1989.

Delaney, G. *In Your Dreams: Falling, Flying, and Other Dream Themes.* New York: HarperCollins Publishers, 1997.

Dement, W. "The Effect of Dream Deprivation." *Science,* 131 (3415), 1705-1707, 1960.

Edgson, V., & Marber, I. *The Food Doctor: Healing Foods for Mind and Body.* New York: Sterling Publishing Co., 1999.

Eigen, M. "Comments on Snake Symbolism and Mind-body Relations." *The American Journal of Psychoanalysis,* 41 (1), 73-79, 1981.

Erikson, E. *Young Man Luther: A Study in Psychoanalysis and History.* New York: W.W. Norton & Company, 1958.

Erikson, E. *Identity and the Life Cycle.* New York: W.W. Norton & Company, 1959.

Foulkes, D. "Dream Reports from Different Stages of Sleep." *Journal of Abnormal and Social Psychology,* 65 (1), 14-25, 1962.

Foulkes, D. "Dreams of the Male Child: Four Case Studies." *Journal of Child Psychology and Psychiatry,* 8, 81-97, 1967.

Foulkes, D. "Children's Dreams: Age Changes and Sex Differences." *Waking and Sleeping,* 1, 171-174, 1977.

Foulkes, D. *Children's Dreams: Longitudinal Studies.* New York: John Wiley & Sons, 1982.

Freud, S. *The Interpretation of Dreams.* New York: Avon Books, 1965.

Gackenbach, J. & Bosveld, J. *Control Your Dreams.* New York: Harper & Row, 1989.

Gackenbach, J. "A Validation of Lucid Dreaming in School Age Children." *Lucidity,* 10 (1), 250-254, 1991.

Garfield, P. *Your Child's Dreams.* New York: Ballantine Books, 1984.

Garfield, P. *The Healing Power of Dreams.* New York: Simon & Schuster, 1991.

Globus, G. G. *Dream Life, Wake Life: The Human Condition Through Dreams.* Albany: State University of New York Press, 1987.

Goodale, M. A. "Active Minds, Sleeping Bodies." *Lancet, 344* (8929), 1036-1037, 1984.

Hall, C. S. & Van de Castle, R. L. *The Content Analysis of Dreams.* New York: Meredith Publishing Company, 1966.

Hamilton-Parker, C. *The Hidden Meaning of Dreams.* New York: Sterling Publishing Co. Inc, 1999.

Hartmann, E. *The Sleep Book.* Glenview: Scott, Foresman and Company, 1987.

Hartmann, E. *Dreams and Nightmares: The Origin and Meanings of Dreams.* Cambridge: Perseus Publishing, 1998.

Haskell, R. "Dreaming, Cognition, and Physical Illness: Part I & Part II." *The Journal of Medical Humanities and Bioethics,* 6, 46-56, 109-122, 1985.

Hilgard, E. R. *Divided Consciousness: Multiple Controls in Human Thought and Action.* New York: Wiley Interscience, 1977.

Holloway, G. *The Complete Dream Book: Discover What Your Dreams Tell About You and Your Life.* Naperville: Sourcebooks, Inc., 2001

Horgan, J. " Lucid Dreaming Revisited." *Omni, 11,* 44-49, 1994.

Horowitz, M. J. "Psychic Trauma." *American General Psychiatry,* 20, 552-559, 1969.

Hunt, H. T. "Some Relations Between the Cognitive Psychology of Dreams and Dream Phenomenology." *The Journal of Mind and Behavior, 7* (2), 213-228, 1986.

James, J. W., & Friedman, R. *When Children Grieve.* New York: HarperCollins, 2001.

Jung, C. K. *Memories, Dreams, Reflections.* New York: Vintage Books, 1989.

Kaplan, C. C. *The Woman's Book of Dreams: Dreaming as a Spiritual Practice.* Hillsboro: Beyond Words Publishing, Inc., 1999

Krippner, S., & Hughes, W. "Dreams and Human Potential." *Journal of Humanistic Psychology,* 10, 1-20, 1970.

Krippner, S., & Ullman, M. "Telepathy and Dreams: A Controlled Experiment with Electrocephalogram-electro-oculogram Monitoring." *Journal of Nervous & Mental Disease,* 151, 394-403, 1970.

LaBerge, S., & Rheingold, H. *Exploring the World of Lucid Dreaming.* New York: Ballantine Books, 1990.

Leach, P. *Your Baby & Child.* New York: Alfred A. Knopf, 2000.

Lohff, D. C. *The Running Press Cyclopedia: Dreams.* Philadelphia: Running Press Book Publishers, 2000.

Milligan, I. L. *Understanding the Dreams You Dream: Biblical Keys for Hearing God's Voice in the Night.* Shippensburg: Treasure House Books, 1997.

Nadis, S. "The Man Who Fought with Squirrels in His Sleep: Odd Things Happen When the Dreamer Is Awake (and Vice Versa)." *Omni,* 16 (11), 12, 1994.

Owens, J., & Millman, R. "Sleep Terrors in a 5-year-old Girl." *Archives of Pediatrics & Adolescent Medicine,* 153, 309-312, 1999.

Pagel, J. F. "Nightmares and Disorders of Dreaming." *American Family Physician,* 61, 2037-2042, 2000.

Papalia, D. E. *A Child's World: Infancy Through Adolescence,* 7th ed. New York: McGraw-Hill, Inc, 1996.

Pearce, J. *Baby & Toddler Sleep Program: How to Get Your Child to Sleep Through the Night Every Night.* Tucson: Fisher Books, 1997.

Peck, M. S. *People of the Lie.* New York: Touchstone, 1998.

Piaget, J. *Play, Dreams and Imitation in Childhood.* New York: W. W. Norton & Company, 1962.

Piaget, J. *The Child's Conception of the World.* Patterson: Littlefield, Adams, 1963.

Piaget, J., & Inhelder, B. *The Psychology of the Child.* New York: Basic Books, 2000.

Pitcher, E. G., & Prelinger, E. *Children Tell Stories: An Analysis of Fantasy.* New York: International Universities Press, Inc, 1963.

Punamaki, R. "The Relationship of Dream Content and Changes in Daytime Mood in Traumatized Vs. Non-traumatized Children." *Dreaming,* 9 (4), 40-55, 1999.

Rechtschaffen, A. "The Single-mindedness and Isolation of Dreams." *Sleep,* 1, 97-109, 1978.

Reed, H. "Learning to Remember Dreams." *Journal of Humanistic Psychology,*13 (3), 33-48, 1973.

Rossi, E. L. "Growth, Change and Transformation in Dreams." *Journal of Humanistic Psychology,*11, 147-169, 1971.

Scallion, G. *Notes From the Cosmos.* W. Chesterfield: Matrix Institute Inc., 1997.

Sechrist, E. *Dreams: Your Magic Mirror.* New York: Cowles Education Corporation, 1968.

Siegel, A. *Dreams That Can Change Your Life: Navigating Life's Passages Through Turning Points Dreams.* New York: Putnam, 1996.

Siegel, A. & Bulkeley, K. *Dreamcatching: Every Parent's Guide to Exploring and Understanding Children's Dreams and Nightmares.* New York: Random House, 1998.

Simonton, O. C., Matthews-Simonton, S., & Creighton, J. L. *Getting Well Again.* New York: Bantam Books, 1981.

Spurr, P. *Understanding Your Child's Dreams.* New York: Sterling Publishing, 1999.

Tholey, P. "Techniques for Inducing and Manipulating Lucid Dreams." *Perceptual and Motor Skills,* 57, 79-90, 1983.

Tholey, P. "Psychotherapeutic Application of Lucid Dreaming." In J. Gackenbach & S. LaBerge (Eds.), *Conscious Mind, Sleeping Brain: Perspectives on Lucid Dreaming.* New York: Plenum, 1988.

Thomson, S. A. *Cloud Nine: A Dreamer's Dictionary.* New York: Avon Books, 1994.

Thurston, M. *How to Interpret Your Dreams: Practical Techniques Based on the Edgar Cayce Approach.* Virginia Beach: A.R.E. Press, 1978.

Thurston, M. *Dreams: Tonight's Answers for Tomorrow's Questions.* San Francisco: Harper & Row, 1988.

Van de Castle, R. L. "Animal Figures in Dreams: Age, Sex, and Cultural Differences." *American Psychologist,* 21, 623, 1966.

Van de Castle, R. L. *Our Dreaming Mind.* New York: Ballantine Books, 1994.

Warnes, H., & Finkelstein, A. "Dreams That Precede a Psychosomatic Illness." *Canadian Psychiatric Association Journal*, 16, 317-325, 1971.

Warren, N. C. *Making Anger Your Ally*. Colorado Springs: Focus on the Family Publishing, 1990.

Wiseman, A. S. *Nightmare Help: A Guide for Parents and Teachers*. Berkeley: Ten Speed Press, 1986.

Author Profile: Janet S. Gould

Janet S. Gould has been interested in dreams ever since she was a child. Her first memory was at the age of six when she woke herself up by talking in her sleep. She would often jerk awake from a nightmare or remember some strange experience she had during the night. As an adult, she began to research what these dreams meant. Always fascinated, she says, "the more I learned, the more I wanted to learn." She is still learning, as there is always something new going on in the study of dreams. She has been recording her own dreams for 30 years and still has a clear memory of several childhood dreams.

Gould holds an M. A. in Transpersonal Studies from Atlantic University with extensive training in all aspects of dreamwork. For over a decade, she has taught classes on working with dreams and has led numerous dream support groups. She spends her time writing and conducting private dream counseling sessions.

Gould also holds a Bachelor of Science Degree in Behavioral Science from Our Lady of Holy Cross College and is a member of the Association for the Study of Dreams, the Association for Research and Enlightenment, and the National Sleep Foundation. She is currently working on two other book projects: *Slumbertime: A Parent's Guide for Children's Sleep* and *Blue Moon: A Parent's guide for Children's Meditation.*

Writing *Catching the Dream: A Parent's Guide for Children's Dreams* has been a true learning experience for Gould. She emphasizes that while many people believe that adult and children's dreams are the same, they are not the same at all. She feels that this book will guide parents (and other adults) to help children get the most out of their dreams.

November 2006

PEARSON PUBLISHING COMPANY
CORPUS CHRISTI, TEXAS

For a complete list and description of our publications and to order books please go to our website:

www.PearsonPub.US

Catching the Dream: A Parent's Guide to Children's Dreams
        By Janet S. Gould

Deal Me In
        By Alyce Guynn with illustrations by Jesse Taylor $23.95

His Angels Are In Charge
        By Frances Cotten Woodard $24.95

Beyond These Eyes
        By Nicole Niewoehner

The Sacred Gifts
        By Katherine Jagoe Massey

Slumbertime: A Parent's Guide for Children's Sleep and Sleep Problems
        By Janet S. Gould

Whale Motel and the Floating Zoo
        By Danice Sweet

For pricing go to our website.

To mail in orders, send (1) a list of titles with number of copies of each title, (2) check or money order for total retail price of all books, plus (3) $5.00 shipping and handling for each book, and (4) your name and mailing address printed clearly, to:

Pearson Publishing Company
711 N. Carancahua, Suite 119
Corpus Christi, Texas 78475